Walks
in the
Western Isles

Walks in the
Western Isles

from Butt to Barra

Mary Welsh

Maps and illustrations by
David Macaulay

First published Westmorland Gazette, 1993
Revised Edition Published by Clan Books, 1999

ISBN 1 873597 10 X

Clan Book Sales Ltd
Clandon House
The Cross, Doune
Perthshire
FK16 6BE

Printed by
Cordfall Ltd, Glasgow

Introduction

The Western Isles lie off the north-western coast of Scotland and stretch for 130 miles from the Butt of Lewis to Barra Head. Here the walker in search of tranquillity and solitude can wander all day over dramatic hills and awesome moorland enjoying the magnificent seascapes without meeting another person.

Lewis

The largest of the western islands, Lewis is made up of rolling moors pitted with freshwater lochs and gouged by long inland sea lochs. It has low hills to the south west, glorious sands and cliffs along its indented west coast and great seascapes on its east coast, with views to the Sutherland hills.

Harris

Linked to Lewis by a range of hills, Harris is a land of high mountains with barely a cupful of soil. It has spectacular waterfalls, hidden lochs and miles of magnificent sands, behind which stretch the machair, unbelievably beautiful with a myriad of summer flowers.

North Uist

The countryside of North Uist consists of heather moorland surrounding innumerable lochs. These are brilliantly revealed from the tops of the hills that form its rocky spine. The east coast is riven with sea lochs and there is a wonderful view of the Isle of Skye. To the west lie great beaches of shell-sand. Man has enjoyed this island for 4,000 years.

Benbecula

A flat land of heathery peat moors, Benbecula barely seems to hold fast its numerous sea and freshwater lochs. Its coasts are indented and there are many sandy beaches. From the nearest mountain it looks as if with one big tide the island might float out to sea. It is sandwiched between the two Uists and linked to them by causeways.

South Uist

South Uist is the second longest island of the Outer Hebrides. Its west coast is one long sandy beach, rarely breached. Behind the sand stretches a wide machair, ideal for farming and crofting. Between the machair and its mountainous spine lies a peaty moorland pocked with freshwater lochs. Its east coast is pierced by three large sea lochs, Boisdale, Eynort and Skipport.

Barra

This lovely island's main centre is Castlebay. The houses, shops, community school, churches, hotels and library nestle on the edge of a huge natural harbour. A few yards offshore, on a small island, stands Kiessimul Castle — the home of the chief of the MacNeils. The glorious sands of the Eoligarry peninsula are famous for their cockles, and the island's airport is here.

Acknowledgment

My thanks go to Maureen Fleming, who helped me research the walks and who, together with my border collie Cami, formed my support team; to Tom, my husband, who gave me much encouragement; and to David Macaulay, who once again has illustrated my walks in Scotland with such a sure and sympathetic touch.

Map of Western Isles

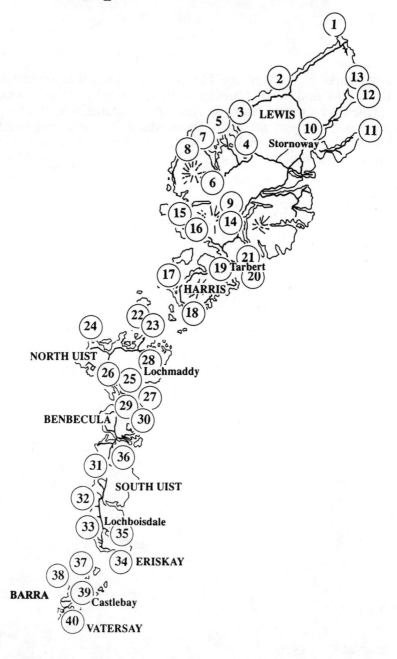

Contents

Contents (continued)

1. A Circular Walk to the Butt of Lewis, visiting a Standing Stone and a Dun on the way

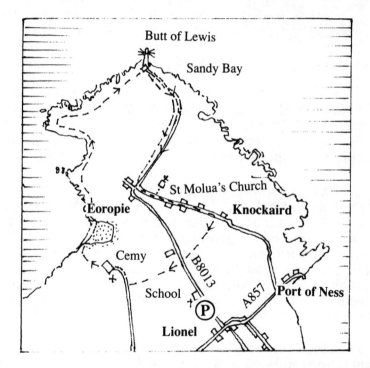

Leave Stornoway by the A857 heading north west across the rolling moors. On reaching the west coast, drive north to pass through Barvas and Upper Barvas. Continue to Ballantrushal and take the signposted left turn for the standing stone, Clach

9

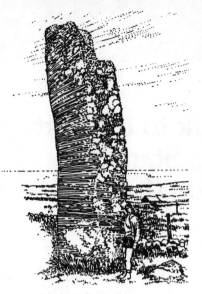

an Truiseil. Follow the road as it swings left and park in the sign-posted car park. You cannot fail to see the stone for it is the largest monolith in the north of Scotland. It is heavily encrusted with lichen. As you look at it, ponder on how it could have been levered into position by ancient folk without the help of modern equipment.

Drive on to the next township, Shader, and look right to see the dun, an ancient defensive structure, on a small island in Loch an Dùin. Notice the stones that form a sketchy causeway to the island.

Clach an Truiseil

Continue along the A857 to the village of Lionel and turn left onto the B8013. Drive a hundred yards to park close to the church or Lionel old school. In the latter, you can visit the Ness Heritage Centre to see the splendid exhibits and displays on local history of the Ness area.

From the old school, walk down the road and turn left just beyond the police station. Look for the yellow balsam growing in a ditch. Continue past the school, along a fenced grassy track. Pass through the gate and ahead to the next gate, walking the grassy sward, which is colourful with summer flowers. On joining a tarmac road, turn right to walk along it as it crosses the machair, a mass of colourful flowers. The track leads to the cemetery — placed, like so many on Lewis, on a slope close to the sea.

Stroll beside the cemetery and on to pass the radio mast. Turn right (north) and walk around the lovely sandy bay of Eoropie, where the great dark-blue Atlantic rollers turn to white foaming surf. Look for the natural arch in the jutting headland, known as the eye of the Butt of Lewis. Pass through the gate on the far side of the bay and bear left to begin the pleasing walk around the indented coastline, proceeding with much care.

Continue along the low cliffs, where the waves crash onto the rocky shoreline, and climb a stile over the next fence. Oystercatchers sit on rocks, all facing in the same direction, and pipe loudly. Sea thrift colours the sward and mushrooms grow in profusion. Ahead, the cliffs become high and sheer; look for fulmars nesting on the many ledges. Pass through the gate in the next fence and then head left out to the cliffs to view Luchruban. This rocky island was once said to have been inhabited by pygmies in prehistoric times, but it is now thought the tiny bones found there were those of small mammals and birds eaten by a hermit.

Thrift and oystercatcher

Stride over the springy turf and along the cliffs to climb a stile that gives access to the pasture around the Butt, the most northerly point of Lewis. It regularly features in the weather reports from coastal stations that come just before the news on Radio 4. Walk to the lighthouse, which was built of red brick by Thomas Stevenson in 1862. Below the towering light stand the support buildings, painted a brilliant white, with yellow surrounds to windows and doors, the latter painted bright green.

Sit on a rock and enjoy this dramatic point, where great expanses of ocean stretch away to the north, east and west. Pause to watch the numerous seabirds nesting on the awesome cliffs. Here black-backed gulls disgorge food to hungry young, fulmars care tenderly for each other and their grey fluffy youngsters and herring gulls fiercely attack any young bird that strays too close to their own. Shags sit on precarious perches and hang their wings to dry. Gannets fly in large groups just over the top of the waves. All is noise and movement and it is a delight to hear and see it all.

Leave the Butt by the narrow road. Look left to see the interesting folding of the pink Lewisian gneiss, Scotland's most ancient rock. Follow the road as it curves inland and passes

11

through an extensive area of lazy-beds. These were formed, in times gone by, by crofters who dug long straight ditches and piled the soil upon the land between, providing extra soil for their crops and improving drainage.

Continue past a delightful sandy bay and at the cross-roads turn left to pass between the modern houses and bungalows of Eoropie. Outside each stand large stacks of peat, each sod cut in the typical Lewis shape. These are burnt to provide hot water and central heating, and the air is full of the smell of peat.

Look for the sign for St Molua's Church. This ancient tenth century chapel, approached by a gated way over croftland, was restored in 1912. Episcopalian services are occasionally held in the lovely simple building. Go inside and enjoy its peace.

Walk on along the road until you approach the signpost for the township of Knockaird. Here turn right and pass between the houses to a stile to the machair, a riot of colour provided by pink clover, hayrattle, buttercups, self heal and yellow hawkweed. Head on towards the road opposite and pass through a gate to the left of the church hall. Turn left up the road to where you have parked your car.

Information

Distance: *6-7 miles*
Time: *3-4 hours, depending on how long you birdwatch.*
Map: *Landranger 8 reference 520666 (Butt of Lewis)*
Terrain: *Easy walking all the way.*

2. A Circular Walk from the Blackhouse at Arnol

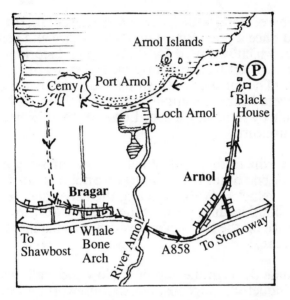

The name blackhouse has been in use since the 1840s. It is used to describe any house in the Western Isles that was constructed with double dry-stone walls and a thatched roof. The last black-houses were built early in this century and some were lived in as late as the 1980s. Now the blackhouses are abandoned and modern bungalows and houses grace the townships.

At the start of this walk visit the blackhouse at Arnol, which is situated just off the A858 on the west coast of Lewis. Go through the main entrance and turn right, as the animals did,

Blackhouse

into the byre. Here, until 19th-century legislation, the dung was removed once a year. Return to the entrance and venture into the barn, which was used for thrashing and storing the grain; and then turn left from the entrance and enjoy the open fire on the floor. The smell of the peat pervades the dwelling and the smoke would have eventually escaped through a hole in the roof made by removing a sod. Look for the box beds and the simple furniture.

For an exhilarating walk along the low cliffs beyond Arnol, park at the end of the road, taking care not to block the turning place for vehicles. Walk on along the cart-track, to the right of a dwelling, leading towards the shore. Pass through a gate in the fence on the left, beyond which grows a large clump of field gentians.

Continue through the gap in the low sod wall, where grow marsh cinquefoil, kingcups, marsh lousewort and silverweed. Make for cliffs overlooking a rocky bay where Atlantic rollers crash white-topped on the jagged rocks. Head left along the cliffs, with the sea to your right, walking over thrifts — and perhaps picking mushrooms for your tea — and on past little Arnol island.

Follow the narrow path that keeps to the right of the fence and runs to the left of a huge spit of boulders stretching across Arnol Bay. In the lea of this large natural breakwater grows a myriad of summer flowers, including great patches of marsh cinquefoil and sea campion. The spit shelters Loch Arnol,

Sea campion and silverweed

with sandbanks emerging above its placid waters. Here several dunlin move deliberately and sedately as they feed — until they chase sandhoppers across the shallows, when their dark legs move furiously. Out on the rocky shore men collect winkles and take them away in their tractors.

Continue behind the spit until you come to the place where it is breached by the River Arnol, flowing out of the loch. Step across on boulders — unless you are walking after several days of rain, in which case you will have to discard your boots and wade. Carry on along the grassy track behind the vast wall of boulders. Cross the narrow road that leads from the shore to Bragar and stroll on along the grassy cliffs.

Walk over the turf, where thrift flowers with lousewort, ragged robin, scabious, mayweed, strawberry-headed clover and hawkweed. Press on to Bragar Bay and move round the end of a fence where it ends on a rock. Follow a narrow path beyond that heads inland with the waters of the bay to your right. This path leads you to the walled cemetery of Bragar. Here you join the narrow, flower-lined road that runs inland to Bragar.

At the T-junction, turn left and walk through the scattered township. Notice the arch on your right made from the huge jawbone of a blue whale that came ashore in 1920. The harpoon that killed it was still attached to its body and is to be seen in the centre of the arch. Walk on to join the A858 and continue ahead for a mile to the signposted left turn to the blackhouse, and so rejoin your car. Before you leave this area, it is well worth visiting the Shawbost School Museum, three miles south along the A858. This folk museum was created by children in a disused church.

Information

Distance: *5 miles*
Time: *3 hours*
Map: *Landranger 8 reference 311495 (blackhouse)*
Terrain: *Easy walking for most of the way. Crossing River Arnol might present problems.*

3. A Circular Walk from the Carloway Broch

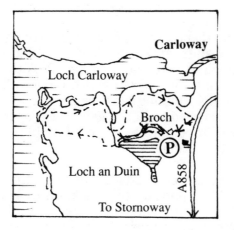

The Carloway Broch dominates the surrounding settlement and land. It seems that wherever you are you can see it and therefore on this walk around the cliffs, where there are no paths, it helps you find your way.

A broch is a circular defensive tower of the early Iron Age in Scotland, and Carloway broch is the best preserved example in the Western Isles. To reach it, leave Stornoway by the A859 and continue on the A858 through Breasclete. After passing Loch an Dùnain and the hotel beyond it, take the next left turn and drive along the road for a quarter of a mile to the parking area and toilets.

Carloway Broch

Cross the road and climb the rough path to pass through the kissing-gate. Wander at will. Notice the double walls that gave strength and stability to the building. Pass through the low entrance and look for the cells between the walls, and for the staircase. A ledge running head-height round the inner wall would have supported a wooden gallery. Enjoy the magnificent view from the broch, with glimpses of blue sea and loch, sparkling in the sunshine.

Return to the car park and walk on along the road to its end by Loch an Dùin, noticing the blackhouses as you go. Once over the culvert at the end, turn right to walk a wide track towards a derelict crofthouse. In the marshy ground on either side flower kingcups, lousewort and cotton-grass. Follow the track as it swings left, and continue ahead, keeping the fence to the right. At the end of the fence, cross a small stream by a stone footbridge and climb straight up the slope of Creag Mhór. At the top there is a breath-taking view of East Loch Roag and of Great and Little Bernera, with their accompanying rocks and tiny islands.

Descend to the greensward on the cliffs below. Turn right, north, and begin a gentle stroll along the cliffs, looking ahead for the easiest and, occasionally, the safest way. Look for bog pimpernel thriving in the damp areas, and field gentians on the drier slopes. Gannets dive into the sea offshore and shags fly from one side of a small bay to another. A pair of falcons leave the jutting rocks of a cliff face and, after several strong wing

18

beats, descend to a rocky outcrop with wings bowed. Look too for mushrooms growing on the sun-warmed slopes.

Bog pimpernel

Continue along the cliffs, keeping the sea to your left, until you come to the headland at the entrance to Loch Carloway. Here is the place to sit to enjoy this lovely stretch of coast. Head further round the cliff tops, with Loch Carloway now to your left. Sheep tracks help you find the easiest way. When you come to a fence, keep to the loch side of it. There is a narrow path outside it as it comes close to a large bay. Where a small landslip has occurred, you can climb the fence by a stile and then climb back over another stile to regain the path beyond the slip.

Stroll on along these glorious low cliffs, where buzzards take off to soar overhead, keening as they go. Look left across the waters of the loch to see the curious stone walls of a field system of a century ago. Carry on until the Carloway pier comes into view. The narrow sheep-track continues to the water's edge, where a stile over the fence gives access to a narrow road. Walk uphill, where the way is bordered with flags, wild mint and ferns.

Look left beyond the dwelling on the left, where you might see the owner Mr MacArthur at his loom. Opposite his blackhouse, pass through a gate. Climb the low hill and then bear left along an old grassy track below cliffs. Continue until you reach a road. Stride ahead and turn right at the end to return to your car.

Information

Distance: *4-5 miles*
Time: *2-3 hours*
Map: *Landranger 13 reference 192412 (broch)*
Terrain: *Easy walking underfoot but hilly. No paths but some useful sheep tracks.*

4. A Circular Walk to the Callanish Stones and Two Stone Circles

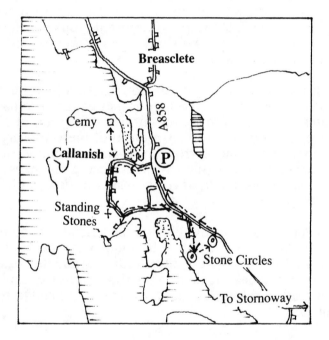

The scattered township of Callanish lies on the A858 just south of Breasclete, 18 miles from Stornoway. The magnificent Standing Stones of Callanish, constructed between 3,000 and 2,000 B.C., are the focal point of the walk.

Park close to the Free Church of Callanish on the A858. Take the well-signposted
side turning that leads west off the main
road. The turning is bordered with eyebright,
hardheads and forget-me-nots. Continue
beside a small arm of East Loch Roag, its
grassy shore covered with sea thrifts. Look
for redshanks, oystercatchers and a solitary
greenshank feeding in the tidal ooze.

Stride up the road where, in a small pasture
pink persicaria, corn marigold and common
hemp nettle flower. At the T-junction turn
right, and follow the narrow road between
several dwellings and out onto heather moorland where marsh lousewort, bog asphodel,
scabious and cotton-grass flourish in the wetter areas. The
narrow road ends at the small walled cemetery belonging to
Callanish. Pause here and enjoy the splendid view up Loch
Roag. A white-painted automatic lighthouse stands on
Greinam island in the blue sea. On the far side of the loch you
can see the factory at Breasclete that produces pharmaceutical
grade oils and beauty care preparations, and the red building
that once housed the families of the Flannan Isles lighthouse.
A pair of hoodie crows fly low over the water.

*Persicaria and
red hemp nettle*

Return to the T-junction and continue ahead, between verges
lined with hay rattle, towards the Stones. What a spectacular
site — 54 stones of Lewisian gneiss stand on a small hill overlooking Loch Roag. Green pastures, with the furrows of earlier
lazy-bed cultivation, stretch away to the rocky outcrops of
slightly higher hills.

The dominant stone stands 15 feet 7 inches and is part of a
circle numbering 13 in all. Within the circle are four upright
stones that once supported a top stone, forming a burial cairn.
From this were recovered fragments of human bone. The circle
is approached by two parallel lines of stones, the north avenue,
composed of 19 stones. There is a western row of four stones
and an eastern and southern row, each of five stones. In 1857-8
Sir James Matheson, a former proprietor of Lewis, had much

Callanish Standing Stones

of the peat removed from around the stones. It had grown to a height of 6 feet 5 inches, obscuring many.

Leave the circle by a side gate and continue along a narrow lane that soon drops to the edge of the loch. Turn right and walk to the small pier at the end of the road to enjoy a pleasing view of islands in Loch Ceann Hulavig.

Return along the narrow road, and past the left turn to the stones. At the A858, turn right, and 100 yards on turn right again. This narrow road leads past several dwellings to a gate to a pasture, which you cross. Pass through the next gate to walk among the stones of a small circle. From here you seem to be in a direct line with the Callanish Stones on their hill.

Look east to see another stone circle on raised ground. A narrow indistinct path leads across the rough, often wet pasture to a stile over a wire fence. Beyond, follow a thin path up the slope to a larger circle of stones. From here you can view both the previous circle and the Callanish Stones.

Walk the path through the heather that continues from the circle to a ladder stile to the side of the A858. Turn left to return to your car.

Information

Distance: *3 miles*
Time: *2 hours*
Map: *Landranger 13 reference 214330 (Callanish Stones)*
Terrain: *Easy walking. Could be wet between the two small circles.*

5. A Circular Walk from Bosta Sands on the Island of Great Bernera

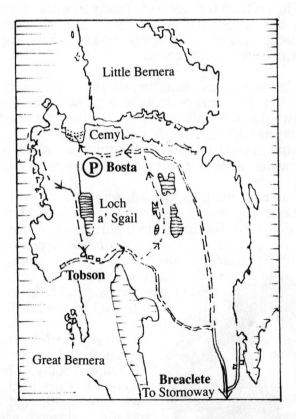

Little Bernera

Cemy

Ⓟ Bosta

Loch
a' Sgail

Tobson

Great Bernera

Breaclete
To Stornoway

Great Bernera, situated in Loch Roag off the west coast of
Lewis, is reached by a narrow but very sturdy white-painted

bridge built in 1953. The island is 25 miles from Stornoway and is approached by taking the A858 to Garynahine and then driving along the B8011. The B8059 leads off on the right, signposted Earshader, to the bridge. Continue ahead to the township of Breaclete and then follow the directions to The Shore. There is a good car park, with excellent toilets, above the glorious sands. A notice says no dogs are allowed.

Enjoy the greensward spangled with buttercups and marsh marigolds, with ragged robin and self heal flowering among the golden haze. Walk down the slope past the walled cemetery of Bosta and on past boulders, where wheatears flit, to the silvery sands. The brilliant turquoise sea gently laps the fine sand and the little bay is sheltered by the island of Little Bernera and several huge jagged rocks. Only oystercatchers disturb the tranquillity of this idyllic corner.

Head left across the sands and climb the grassy cliffs, with their many rocky outcrops, to walk to the headland. The turf is a botanist's paradise with lousewort, sea thrift, spotted orchis, heather, eyebright, lady's bedstraw and the pretty bog pimpernel growing in great profusion. Continue round the headland with the waters of West Loch Roag now below to your right.

Walk on over the high ground, scrambling easily over the rocks. Look for roseroot growing in crevices of boulders, gannets diving for fish in the deep blue waters of the sea loch and kittiwakes nesting on the precipitous cliffs. Cairns on the highest hills give you some help in finding your way, but it is very pleasing to find your own way, with the sea to your right to stop you feeling lost.

Kittiwakes

When you reach a sturdy wall, turn left and walk beside it, climbing steadily. Then drop downhill towards Loch a'Sgail, where you will find a small metal gate through which you pass. Continue ahead through another gate in the fence. Beyond strike diagonally right to pass through a further gate in the next fence. Look for bogbean, lobelia and marsh cinquefoil flourishing in a small loch. Press on, taking a right diagonal over a marshy area where sundew, marsh lousewort and bog asphodel flower. Descend a rocky cliff with care to a gate in the far right corner of a fence.

Step out across the pasture to a white painted gate and pass between the ruins of two blackhouses. Continue to a metal gate. Beyond, walk the path, which leads to another gate and gives

Blackhouse ruins at Tobson

access to a road and the settlement of Tobson. Here, turn left and walk the road that follows the curve of the bay. Just before the top of the slope, pass through a gate in the fence on the left.

Head right towards a dwelling with blue paint and then on, keeping to the left of it. Traverse the lazy-beds behind the house and then bear left to ascend a wide grassy gully between two long rocky ridges. At the top, pass through a gate on the right. Drop down the slope to the side of another sturdy wall, and follow this to a gate, through which you pass. Beyond, large white water lilies float on a cobalt blue loch.

Continue uphill beside the wall, now on your right. Follow it as it descends to another loch. Turn left and, keeping a little up the slope, walk ahead parallel to the loch until you reach another wall. Stride ahead, keeping to the left of the wall. Step across a narrow stream and walk on; below lies Loch na Muilne. On the island in the middle of the loch black-headed gulls sit snoozing in the afternoon sun.

Press on in the same direction, picking the driest way. Look for the many ruins of what must have been a large settlement two centuries ago. When you reach the road, turn left and walk downhill to rejoin your car.

Information

Distance: 4 miles
Time: 3 hours
Map: Landranger 13 reference 138400 (Bosta car park)
Terrain: No paths. Find your own way over moorland turf, sometimes wet, and rocky outcrops that give your boots good purchase.

6. A Linear Walk to the Beehive Dwellings below Scalaval Hill

Little Loch Roag

B8011

P

Loch Morsgail

Beehive
Dwellings

Scalaval

No one seems to know what these ancient beehive-shaped structures were used for. They are situated in a pleasing hollow, close to a feeder stream that joins the River Abhainn a' Lòin below the rocky slopes of Scalaval. To reach them you will need determination, and at times you will have a wet walk.

Leave Stornoway by the A858. Turn left at Garynahine onto the B8011 and continue to the head of Little Loch Roag. Park on the west side of the bridge where the road makes a hairpin bend. Cross the road from the lay-by and pass through the gate, which carries a notice saying it is a private road and no dogs are allowed. Walk the access track towards Morsgail Lodge, a reinforced way that runs beside a hurrying peat-stained burn. Overhead a buzzard is mobbed by a large number of starlings. A pair of herons feed leisurely in the river, unperturbed by the drama above.

The track passes first through moorland and then through scattered rhododendrons and gorse bushes. Continue between alders, birch, willow and conifers, a welcome relief from the addictive but bleak Lewis scenery. The track curves gracefully and Morsgail Lodge lies ahead. A notice directs walkers to the left, over a bridge. This crosses the burn just below the weir at the foot of Loch Morsgail. Walkers are asked not to use the road to the lodge.

From now on the way is wet. Follow a wide peaty track made by a moorland terrain vehicle. Though this has churned the ground, it has found the best way. The track runs on gentle slopes above Loch Morsgail. Continue to the head of the loch and pass through the gate close to the wind-rippled water. Cross a tiny stream on a stone slab and then walk beside the loch until you come to the bridge over the Abhainn a' Lòin. Do not cross but continue upstream, following the tractor route or a sheep-track closer to the burn.

In a small hollow by the fast-flowing burn, a clump of rowans are laden with red berries. Press on to where the river swings away to the right and you can see the buttresses of a broken bridge. Here look for a good track that soon becomes dry. This winds on, with the rocky slopes of Scalaval to the left. Walk on along this track for nearly a mile and the beehive dwellings stand just where it drops down to the stream — where white lousewort grows. Pause here for as long as you can and then retrace your outward journey.

Beehive dwellings — interior

Information

Distance: 6 miles
Time: *3 hours*
Map: *Landranger 13 reference 140238 (parking)*
Terrain: *Metalled road for a third of the way and then a wet moorland route.*

7. A Circular Walk from Kneep via Berie Sands

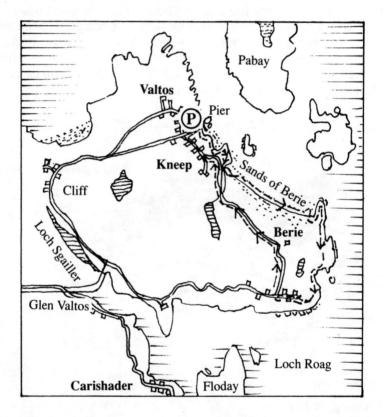

To reach Kneep, leave Stornoway as for Walk 6. Continue on the B8011 along the west side of Little Loch Roag and Loch Roag. Just before the start of Glen Valtos, turn right and head north beside Loch Sgailler. Pass through the settlement of Cliff. From here you can drive to the car park overlooking the sands. The sands are beautiful but unsafe for swimming. Press on to Kneep and park close to the phone box, choosing a place that does not impede other vehicles.

Stroll down the narrow road, opposite the phone box, to the small pier. Turn right to walk south-east across the sandy bay, which is sheltered by the islands of Pabay and Shiaram. Here, ringed plover and dunlin race over the sand after prey. If the tide is high you may have to walk the shore road, which you join just before the last two dwellings at the end of the bay.

After passing the last house, turn left to climb the cliff, keeping to the right of the fence. Here on the cliff top a magnificent carpet of flowers delights the eye. Look for deep purple orchis, harebells, lady's bedstraw, field gentians, self heal, hayrattle, frog orchid and meadow rue. Continue along the cliff edge, keeping beside the fence. In a sandy hollow to the right, a pair of ringed plover solicitously care for their young, as yet only small balls of fluff but with their ring markings already visible.

Descend the slopes to reach the extensive silver sands of Berie, which are protected from the Atlantic rollers by the

Berie Sands

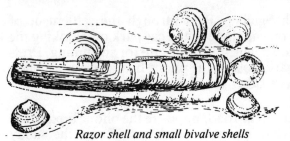
Razor shell and small bivalve shells

island of Vacsay. Look for the razor shells and the tiny delicate pink shells of a bivalve that litter the bay. The sound of the waves lapping the lovely shore is diminished by the screeching of a large flock of terns that remain close to their breeding site on the dunes and sands. Young eiders swim just off shore and a merganser marshals her young as they bob on the waves.

Press ahead to the towering rock of the cliff at the end of the wonderful sands and climb right to a stile over a fence. Walk up the slope and bear left to look across Loch Roag to the island of Vuia, with Great Bernera beyond. Head on along the cliffs and pass a tiny bay where the water turns to aquamarine over the sand. Go on around the headland to another sandy bay where curlews feed and a black guillemot swims sedately on the waves. Continue onwards, climbing up a damper gully where sundew, cotton-grass and marsh lousewort flourish. Follow the cliffs round, always keeping the sea loch to the left, until you reach a fence. Pass through the gate in line with a dwelling. Bear slightly left to a second gate and then right to a third to the start of a narrow road at Reef.

Walk the road with the loch to your left. Turn right at the T-junction and walk ahead, soon leaving the dwellings behind. Enjoy walking the lonely road, which passes through rocky outcrops. Continue to the sands of Berie. Here you may wish to continue on the road to rejoin your car, or you may be tempted to walk the sands and cliff before returning to the road at the start of Kneep.

Information

Distance: 5 miles
Time: 3 hours
Map: Landranger 13 reference 100358 (Berie Sands)
Terrain: Easy walking all the way.

8. A Circular Walk from Uig Sands, West Lewis

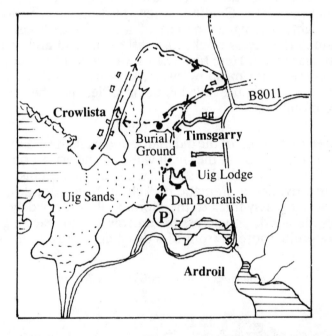

This walk takes you across two stretches of the glorious sands of Uig and can be attempted only when the tide is out. Leave Stornoway by the A858. Turn left at Garynahine onto the B8011 and continue alongside Little Loch Roag. Follow the road through Glen Valtos and on through the settlement of Ardroil. Beyond, the road to the shore is well signposted. Pass through the gate at the end of the road and park close to the toilets.

Walk down the track. In sand dunes to the left lady's mantle grows among the marram grass. Reaching the great expanse of silvery sand, stride ahead across the bay where oystercatchers feed in the burn that flows out of Loch Stacsavat. On a green hill stands Uig Lodge, the house where Arthur Ransome of *Swallows and Amazons* fame came to recuperate and recover from a writing block.

Bear slightly left towards a sturdy bridge, built in 1980, which spans the hurrying burn. Walk up the slope and bear left across the short-cropped turf, where harebells grow and wheatears flit among the rocks. Continue a few yards along the shore and turn right, passing to the left of a small crofthouse. Stride on along the access track, turn left at the end and walk to a triangular green. Here turn left to walk a narrow road, which is bordered with meadow sweet, silverweed and red bartsia, towards a guesthouse called Baile-na-Cille, once the manse and a listed building.

Keep to the right of the old manse and walk the grassy sward. Pause here to look at the small walled cemetery set on a green hill. Beyond stretch the sands, with the mountains of West Lewis providing a dramatic backcloth. Stride on, descending an ancient grassy track to the shore. Follow the widely-spaced rocks that guide you across the narrow bay to reach a gate on the opposite shore in front of a dwelling, closest to the sands,

The mountains of West Lewis from walled cemetery

34

at Crowlista. In a wet area half-way across a mixed flock of dunlin and ringed plover probe the mud.

Ringed plover and dunlin

Turn right and walk the narrow road above the bay, where primroses flower and green plovers strut regally across the moorland. Climb the slope and continue where the road curves right towards Timsgarry. At the T-junction, turn right, and on to take the next right turn. Stride past the dwellings, the tea room, the school and the church. At the triangle of grass passed earlier, turn left. Walk to the cottage and left beyond. Carry on over the sandy turf to the bridge. Before you cross, walk to a rock causeway at the end of the small cliffs, which leads to the last tiny grassy hillock. Here stands Dùn Borranish, built in the early Iron Age as a communal refuge against invaders.

Return and cross the bridge, and as you dawdle over the sands remember the story behind the find of the famous Norse-carved Lewis chessmen. They were found in a sand bank at Uig in 1831, where legend says they were buried many years before by the murderer of a sailor lad who had brought them ashore from a passing ship. They are now housed in the British Museum.

To rejoin your car, walk up the cart-track.

Always check on the tides.

Information

Distance: *4½ miles*
Time: *2 hours*
Map: *Landranger 13 reference 049329 (parking)*
Terrain: *Easy walking all the way.*

9. A Walk to Loch Langavat, linear or circular

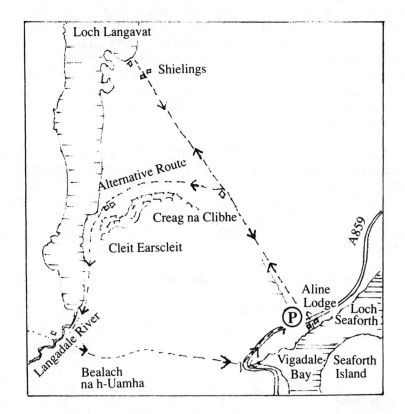

Leave Stornoway by the A859 and head south. After some 11 miles, you may like to turn left at the signposted road to the settlement of Keose and drive to the small harbour. Here seaweed is dried and ground to a powder before it is shipped to the mainland to be used in a variety of foods. Return to the main road and continue south, passing lochs made attractive by white water lilies. Notice the islands in the lochs, lush with plants, bushes and trees. These are able to thrive away from the voracious sheep.

Drive on to Aline Lodge, found at grid reference 197119 on the O.S. map. Look for a row of Scots pine on the left and Seaforth Island, set in Loch Seaforth, also on the left. Just beyond the access road to the dwelling on the shore, there is a small parking area on the right, approached by a rough track and beyond a pair of metal gates. Walk up the reinforced track, climbing steadily. Look back often to enjoy the glorious view along the loch and out to sea.

Moorland stretches away on both sides of the track, and where the way has been maintained you can see how thick the peat can be, ranging from two to eight feet. A buzzard flies high overhead after quartering the heathery slopes. Stags stand high on the tops as if curious at the approach of the walker. Look for the cascading waterfall on the Abhainn a' Mhuil and walk on until you can see the ruins of a shieling away to the left. Shielings provided shelter for shepherds tending their flocks and saved them from having to return to the village each night.

Waterfall on the Abhainn a' Mhuil

37

Here a decision has to be made. Most walkers will wish to continue along the track for one-and-a-half miles, until it reaches the shores of Loch Langavat, where there are more shielings. After enjoying this large mountain-girt loch, you return by the same route.

For those who want a more adventurous route and are strong walkers, unperturbed by a trackless and often wet moorland, it can be satisfying to follow the contours above the loch and pick up another track at the far end. To take this alternative route, strike left (south-west) from the track, across the heather moorland, to the shieling below Creag na Clibhe. When you reach it, look around for several more. Here a pair of handsome stonechats scold from the top of a rocky outcrop and several very dark Hebridean wrens flit from one heather branch to another.

Follow the contours below the steep slopes of Creag na Clibhe and then follow the Clibhe burn down to a grassy hollow on the shore of the loch. Look for more shielings here. Look also for a group of does. Continue south below the steep slopes of Cleit Earscleit to the end of the loch, where red grouse feed on the heather. Then follow the Langa-dale River upstream. To the right on the slopes of Stulaval, you will have your first sighting of an east-west track. Join it beside the river, where the burn was once bridged, turning left to walk the zig-zag route.

Ascend steadily to the pass, Bealach na h-Uamha. Once over the top, the houses by Loch Seaforth come into view, two miles downhill. At the end of the track, turn left and walk the A859 to rejoin your car.

Red grouse in heather

Information

Distance: 7 miles (linear walk)
8½ miles (alternative route)

Time: 3 hours (linear)
          4 hours (alternative)
Map: Landranger 14 reference 197119 (Aline Lodge)
Terrain: Linear walk — good stony track all the way.
          Alternative — strong walking boots required to give
          you purchase over the heather moorland with its rocky
          outcrops.

10. A Circular Walk through Stornoway Woods surrounding Lews Castle

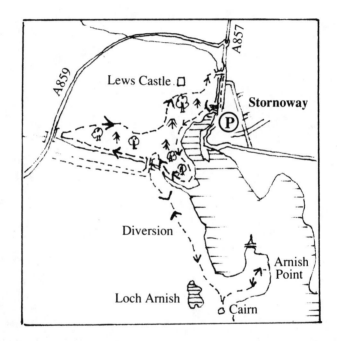

Sir James Matheson bought Lewis from the MacKenzies in 1844. He had made a fortune in the Far East and spent much of his money on building bridges and roads on the island. He also built the mock Tudor building that dominates Stornoway Harbour, known as Lews Castle. Though the castle is not open to the public, the extensive grounds in which it stands are. They are planted with rhododendrons and many species of trees.

To walk in this pleasing wooded area, which contrasts strongly with the remainder of the island, park in Bayhead and walk to the large archway, known as the Porter's Lodge. This is to be found opposite the junction of Matheson Road with Bayhead. Beyond the lodge, turn left and begin the charming walk along a metalled road, which is almost free of traffic. Coming to the harbour basin enjoy a picturesque view of Cromwell Street quay. Continue beneath huge beeches to pass the red-stone castellated castle on the right.

Head on along the road. Look out to sea and notice the treeless area beyond the woods where rocky outcrops emerge from the green turf. Take the right turn, signposted Lady Matheson's monument, and climb to it beneath beech, ash, sycamore and elm. Then return to the road beside the harbour. Here grey seals patiently wait for an easy meal from trawlermen. Continue where the road ceases and a reinforced track climbs steadily above the estuary, bordered with a huge bank of rhododendrons.

Follow the path as it bears right inland for a few yards and then soon returns to the side of the estuary. The path again swings right and inland, keeping close to the River Creed. On the opposite bank a lacy waterfall descends. Walk upstream where, after rain, the peat-stained burn descends in many furious falls.

Continue past a bird bath and drinking fountain and head on to a footbridge. Here you can choose between a longer or shorter walk. To extend your walk, cross the bridge and take another good track through the lovely deciduous woodland to a gate onto heather and bog myrtle moorland. Stroll on to a road where you turn left and head towards the sea, with a good view of the Arnish lighthouse and the Eye peninsula.

Follow the road downhill past Arnish power station, which is pleasingly sited so as not to obtrude on the moorland. Pass Arnish tarn, from where a curlew calls and where common

Gulls and seal

gulls and black-backed gulls preen and snooze in the afternoon sun. When you reach Lewis Offshore Ltd (not so pleasingly sited), turn right and walk uphill to a cairn.

Cairn at Arnish

The cairn marks the place where Prince Charles Edward Stuart, in 1746, waited in vain for a ship from Stornoway. Sit by the cairn and enjoy the dramatic coastline stretching southwards. Inland, ravens congregate on rocky outcrops and croak raucously. From here, return by the same route to the bridge.

If you have chosen the shorter walk, ignore the bridge and continue to a weir where you might see salmon jumping. Look for dippers flying downstream to find shallows for catching prey.

Follow the track as it swings away from the river. Turn left at the division of paths and then quickly right, which brings you out onto heather moorland. Here grows hard fern with fertile fronds. Another dipper flies low across the track from one narrow rocky stream to another.

Stride the track as it continues ahead into more glorious deciduous woodland. Pass Lady Matheson's monument, now to your right, and walk on to pass the castle, also to your right. A hundred yards along, take a path that heads right and on through trees. Descend some concrete steps and cross the road to a footbridge over the harbour. Walk ahead and turn left along Bayhead to rejoin your car.

Information

Distance: *4 miles or 7 miles*
Time: *Several hours, depending on how long you sit on the many well-placed seats!*
Map: *Landranger 8 reference 425337 (Porter's Lodge)*
Terrain: *Easy walking all the way.*

11. A Visit to a Ruined Church and a Circular Walk on Tiumpan Head

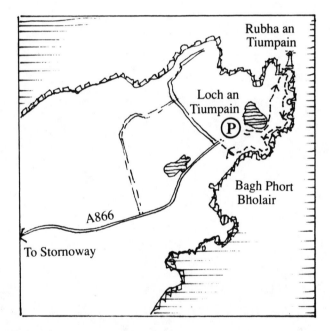

An Rubha, or the Eye peninsula, juts out into the sea to the east of Stornoway. It is almost an island, the A866 access road crossing an isthmus protected from the huge waves of the Minch by strong sea walls.

Ruins of St Columba's Church

To reach the peninsula, leave Stornoway by the A866 to cross the thin strip of land and park in the signposted lay-by just before the sign for Aiginis. Turn left, pass through a kissing-gate and walk on. Follow the track, bearing to the right. Pass through a metal gate and then another kissing-gate to visit the ruins of St Columba's Church, one of the most important religious sites on Lewis. The church was built on the site of a cell occupied by the Celtic saint Catan in the seventh century. It is said that 19 chiefs of the Macleods of Lewis are buried here.

After visiting the ruins, and if the tide is low, you can walk the golden sands, where terns congregate in vast numbers on the island of Langa Sgeir Mhór. There are good views across Broad Bay to the rugged eastern coastline of Lewis.

Return to the car and continue on the A866 for a further six miles; where the A road makes a sharp turn left, proceed ahead along the narrow road to Tiumpan Head. Park in a large lay-by beside Loch an Tiumpan. Here, on the tranquil waters, young mallards, eiders and tufted ducks feed quietly. A heron, rising slowly from the

Ducks feed quietly on tranquil waters

45

fringing reeds, flies low over the water to settle in another reed bed further round the loch.

Walk on along the narrow road, which ends at Tiumpan Head lighthouse. From here there are magnificent views across the Minch to mainland Scotland. Large colonies of fulmars and kittiwakes nest on the huge cliffs and stacks.

Return along the road for 50 yards and then walk left over the grassy cliffs. Enjoy the heather and scabious-covered turf, with the Minch to your left. Follow the indented coastline with care, always moving inland if you feel too close to the edge. Huge rock faces slope down to the sea, the upper parts clad with brilliant orange lichen. Look for sundew, orchis and lousewort in the wetter areas. Gannets dive for fish in the Minch, terns fly overhead, an oystercatcher sunbathes on a rock and a guillemot swims sedately on the swelling water.

Continue to Bholair Bay, where a fisherman casts out his net into the water. Join a narrow road and follow it as it swings right to walk inland. At the crossroads, turn right to rejoin your car beside the loch.

Information

Distance: *3 miles*
Time: *1½ hours*
Map: *Landranger 8 reference 575378 (lighthouse)*
Terrain: *Easy walking all the way.*

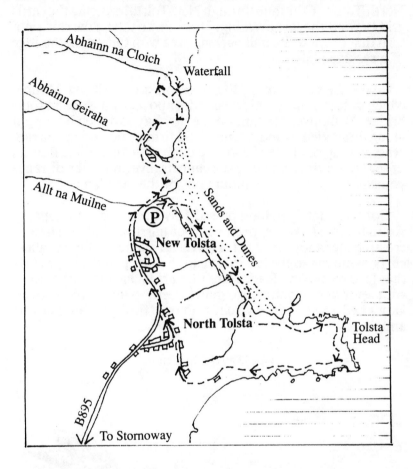

12. A Circular Walk from the Tràigh Mhór via Tolsta Head

This is a walk for times when the tide is out and you can walk the mile and a half of silver sand and perhaps leave the only footsteps to be seen.

47

Leave Stornoway by the A857 and turn right at Newmarket onto the B895. Drive through Tunga, Col, Bac, Griais and North Tolsta. Continue through New Tolsta, crossing the cattle grid beyond the last dwelling. Drive on to take a narrow right turn that drops to a small parking area with toilets, on the edge of a secluded bay.

Leave the car park by the stile and cross Allt na Muilne, which descends in foaming cascades above, by a wooden footbridge. Walk over the sand of the tiny bay and then bear right along the golden strand. Dunes, held firm by flowering marram grass, rise up on the land side and close to these the lilac flowers of sea rocket thrive. Out to sea gannets dive and in the distance you can see, faintly, the mountains of the mainland.

Continue until you have passed Tolsta cemetery, on slopes to the right, and have stepped over four narrow, shallow streams crossing the sands to the sea. Then head inland to climb shallow cliffs, swinging to the left to ascend to the top of the huge cliffs that lead to Tolsta Head. Here the turf is one mass of colour, with eyebright, buttercup, hawkweed, pignut, red clover, lady's bedstraw, kidney vetch, scabious, field gentian, ragwort and yarrow.

View from cliff top, Tolsta

When you reach the fence that crosses the headland from inland to the cliff edge, head right to pass through a gate and then return nearer to the cliff edge. Walk with care along the top, keeping a safe and comfortable distance. Here the sward changes and the rough grass is sparsely carpeted with moorland flowers. From the cliffs come the

Fulmar and skua

continual cooing of fulmars, which nest in vast numbers using every available ledge. Close by each pair of adults sits a large ball of grey fluff — their one nestling. Suddenly the noise from the fulmars increases as five skuas, large brown birds with white patches on outspread wings, fly too close to the nesting colony. Look down to the foot of a stack, far below, where a hundred or so eider gather and call.

When, to the right, the lighthouse on the Eye peninsula comes into view, bear right towards it to cut across Tolsta Head. Continue along the cliffs, passing two natural arches. Look for the small pier and the silvery Giordale Sands. A pencil-slim waterfall drops down the cliff.

On reaching a fence, walk inland until you come to a gate. Pass through the gate and stroll along a raised bank that stretches ahead towards a dwelling. Follow the fence right and then left to join a narrow road. Turn right and then right again as you head towards North Tolsta. At the main road, turn right and continue through New Tolsta to rejoin your car.

Information

Distance: *6 miles*
Time: *3 hours*
Map: *Landranger 8 reference 534490 (car park)*
Terrain: *Pleasing walking along the sands. A steady climb to the cliff top where proceed with care.*

13. A Linear Walk from the Tràigh Mhór to the Waterfall on the Burn, Abhainn na Cloich

Leave Stornoway and park just north of New Tolsta, as for Walk 12. Walk back uphill to the heather-bordered road and continue right. As you approach the next glorious sandy bay, move carefully to the cliff edge to see a huge stack, a grass-covered pillar of rock that has become separated from the main cliffs. Here, on precarious ledges, fulmars tend their young, gliding to their nest sites on steady, outstretched wings.

Stride on along the narrow road to a magnificent bridge, 'the Bridge to Nowhere', over the burn, Abhainn Geiraha. It was built by Lord Leverhulme for a road he intended to run to Ness but which was never built. The burn, white-topped and peat-stained, races through a ravine where grow honeysuckle, willow, heather, bracken and several aspen trees. Savour this glorious lush corner.

At the bridge the tarmac ceases and a reinforced track continues out onto moorland; to the right there is a good view to the sandy bay and the stack. From the tops of bracken come the sweet notes, often repeated, of the stonechat. Look for its black head and white collar and shoulder patch, contrasting with the rich brown of its breast. Head on until you have a first sighting of the dramatic waterfall, the main object of the walk.

Stonechat on bracken stem

*Waterfall on
Abhainn na Cloich*

Carry on along the track until it peters out at the remains of a concrete structure by which you can cross the burn. Turn right and follow a narrow path over the heather moorland to the side of the falls. Sit on a rock and enjoy the foaming skirt of water that plummets over water-blackened rocks into a deep pool. Here the wind catches the burn and tosses spray into the air, filling the top of the ravine. The burn hurries on in lacy cascades and then, under aspen, descends once more in white-topped falls.

Here you may wish to return by the path taken earlier to rejoin the track. Or, if the burn is not too high, you may prefer to drop down on a narrow path, through bracken, to cross the burn on boulders, or to wade across. Then ascend the slope to regain the road for your return to the car park.

Information

Distance: 4 miles
Time: 2 hours
Map: Landranger 8 reference 538508 (waterfall)
Terrain: Easy road and track walking all the way except for the short
*   path to the waterfall and the scrambling up the hillside.*

14. A Circular Walk starting by the Vigadale Burn and returning by Scaladale

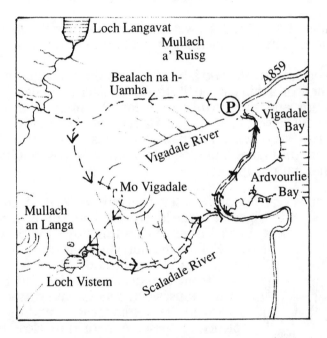

Park on a verge on the A859 at Vigadale burn (grid reference 186115), making sure you do not use a passing place or obstruct access. Walk up the track that runs through Vigadale Glen to the cairn at the pass Bealach na h-Uamha. Take the path that bears to the left. After a few yards, to avoid losing height, leave the path and walk left over the heather moorland. There is no

View from Mullach an Langa

path and the hill slopes are wet in places. Make for the top of Mò Vigadale, from where there is a dramatic view of Loch Langavat.

If you are a strong and adventurous walker you can carry on from here on a thin path to the top of Mullach an Langa, Mulla-fo-thuath and even Mulla-fo-dheas. From here there are wonderful views of West Loch Tarbert and the islands of Soay Mòr and Soay Beag. The path continues round the ridge to Clisham, the highest point on the island of Harris, but the way is somewhat precipitous.

If, however, you prefer a less energetic walk, descend from Mò Vigadale to the lovely loch in the mountain fastness, Loch Vistem. From this flows the Scaladale River. Follow the hurrying burn as it descends through heather moorland, where wheatears flit from boulder to boulder and butterwort, lousewort, sundew and cotton-grass grow in the wetter areas — and there are plenty of these. A path runs close to the river and this should help you on your way, though it is wet in places and requires some boulder-hopping.

Sundew and cotton-grass

The path reaches the A859 at the Scaladale Bridge. Here turn left and walk a mile to rejoin your car.

54

Information

Distance: 7 miles if you leave the ridge at Mò Vigadale
Time: 3-4 hours
Map: Landranger 13 or 14 reference 186115 (Vigadale burn)
Terrain: A wet walk over heather and boulders.

15. A Circular Walk from Hushinish

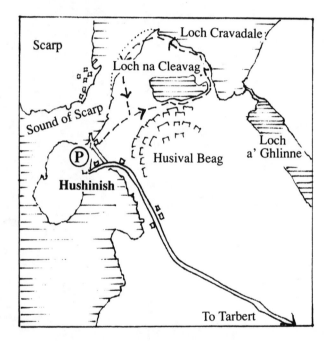

This walk could be considered perfect in that it has cliffs, silver sands, inland and sea lochs, an island, a golden eagle and a glorious machair.

Leave Tarbert by the A859 (north) and take the B887 just north of the town. This road follows a circuitous route along the northern shores of West Loch Tarbert. Pause in a suitable place, a mile along the B road, to look at the chimney of an old whaling station at Bunavoneadar. The station was established before the First World War by Norwegians. In 1922 Lord Leverhulme bought it but by 1930 the venture had proved a complete failure.

Continue along the narrow road, where only passengers can enjoy the views, to park just before the white gates of Amhuinn-suidhe Castle. Walk on to see the lovely falls on the burn that descends from Loch Leosaid. Where the white-topped water enters the sea loch, Loch Leosavay, salmon congregate, their fins parting the water like mini sharks. Regularly, a large fish makes a leap into the air and then another before it begins the seemingly perilous ascent to spawn.

Return to the car and drive further along the road, which passes immediately in front of the castle. This is the property of the proprietor of the North Harris Estate. The castle was built by the Earl of Dunmore in 1868 and it was the Countess, his wife, who restored St Clement's Church at Rodel (Walk 18). A wide lawn fronts the castle and in a castellated wall, over-looking the loch, stand several small cannon. Pass through the arched gateway and continue until you reach the end of the road and the magnificent sandy beach of Hushinish. Here the sea turns to green as it hurries over the shell-sand.

Beginning of the walk

Park on a long narrow lay-by above the beach and take a single-track sandy road that leads off north. It is bordered with a carpet of buttercups and very large deep blue harebells and leads to a small pier from where small boats leave to go to the island of Scarp. Just before the pier, take a track that leads right across a glorious stretch of machair where grow innumerable, colourful flowers. Pass through a gate and walk on along a narrow path through primroses to a stile over a long wall.

Follow the wide, well-made track as it climbs up and up high above the rocky shore where shags, on jagged boulders, dry their wings. Where the track ceases, continue along a narrow path that goes on to swing right. It climbs through a narrow corridor between a mountain on one side and a hill on the other. At the top of the gully, first the sea loch, Loch Cravadale, comes into view, and then Loch na Cleavag, a freshwater loch. The indistinct path hugs the base of the huge side of Husival Beag on the right. Here, out of the reach of hungry sheep, honeysuckle blossoms.

The way continues along the shore of Loch na Cleavag to come to a crofthouse, now the property of a helicopter firm with its own landing pad — totally unexpected in such a remote corner. Pause here in this quiet hollow to look for a golden eagle using the thermals, rising up the side of the mountain. It soars and soars, never flapping its wings once, and is eventually lost to sight over the sea.

Stroll around Loch na Cleavag and cross the narrow strip of land between it and the sea. Here the pounding waves have thrown up a huge barrier of rounded boulders. From these look right (south) to Glen Cravadale, a forbidding U-shaped valley with sheer sides, softened by its reflections in Loch a' Ghlinne.

Walk on to the next great barrier of boulders and then look across to Loch Resort, which is shadowed by high mountains on both *Honeysuckle* sides. This deep, narrow inlet forms the boundary between Harris and Lewis. Stride on along the low grassy cliffs, with the sea to your right, crossing a vast area of lazy-beds, where the pretty centaury grows. Carry on around the cliffs until you reach the wonderful extensive sands of Meilein, which is bordered by high dunes on your left.

From the sands look across Scarp Sound to Scarp itself. From here you can count at least 11 old dwellings and just make out the ruined school and perhaps a church. Beside the latter is a small burial ground. Today only one cottage seems to be occupied.

Stroll to the end of the sands and then strike inland, heading towards the path taken earlier at the start of the gully. Follow the exhilarating path — later a track — to retrace your outward route and rejoin your car.

Information

Distance: *5 miles*
Time: *3 hours*
Map: *Landranger 13 reference 991124 (start of path)*
Terrain: *Generally easy walking. Cliff path a little vertiginous in one part. Gully path can be very wet.*

16. A Linear Walk to the Dam on Loch Chliostair

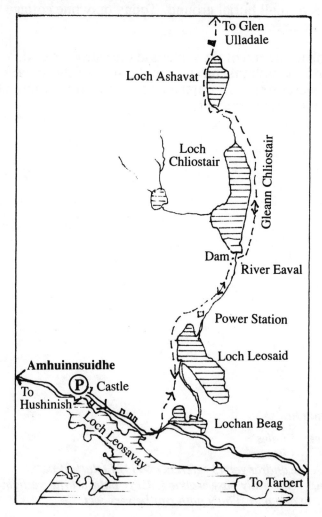

Leave Tarbert by the A859, driving north. Turn left onto the B887 and continue until you reach the gates to Amhuinnsuidhe Castle and the sign for the village. Park just before the gate to the castle. Walk back to take the narrow road signposted Chliostair Power Station. Stride the access road to walk past Lochan Beag on the right. Pass the dramatic waterfall that tumbles out of Loch Leosaid. Beehive-shaped stacks of peat stand drying on both sides of the road. Press onwards for two miles until you reach the unusual arched dam. Beyond, the narrow reinforced path continues beside Loch Chliostair and on into the rugged, lonely mountainous heart of Harris. Walk as far as you wish.

When you return, by the same route, enjoy the magnificent view of the indented coastline and the islands that lie below you. As you approach the road, notice the culverts that once allowed the outlet burn from Loch Leosaid to pass the road. Next to it is the modern version of a culvert.

If you failed to see the salmon leaping from pool to pool on the waterfall tumbling over rocks, described in Walk 15, you might wish to carry on towards the castle and end this walk in this way.

Information

Distance: 5 miles
Time: 2 hours
Map: Landranger 13 reference 069099 (dam)
Terrain: Rough paths and some road walking

17. A Walk to an Old Church and a Climb to the Top of Chaipaval

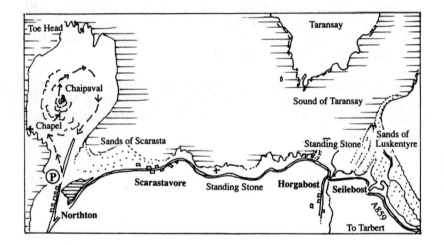

Leave Tarbert, driving south by the A859, passing through some very rocky terrain. Then the road begins its descent towards the west coast with its large expanses of brilliant white sand. Look for the sands of Luskentyre, where the Laxdale River crosses the beach to the sea. Just beyond the dunes, to the south, are the sands of Seilebost.

Head on towards Horgabost, where there are more sands. Once beyond the turning on the left for the township, make for the signposted parking area at the south end of the sandy beach,

Tràigh Iar. (There is a crash barrier and a seat.) From here you can see the Horgabost standing stone on a grassy hill at the far end of the beach. It is easily reached by walking across the sands and climbing the hill. Enjoy the good views across the Sound of Taransay to the fertile and attractive island of Taransay. The island was occupied at the turn of the century but is not now. Nearby an eagle flies across the slopes to a rocky outcrop and sits and surveys the sunny scene, its head and shoulders a soft fawn.

Drive on to the right turn for Northton, a township linked by a spit of land to Chaipaval and Toe Head, and by the houses. Once past the last dwelling, park on the left of the sandy track. Away to the right, beyond the flower-covered machair, stretch the extensive sands of Scarasta. Walk the track and take the left fork where it branches. This leads you over the glorious machair with good views of the sands on the west side of the isthmus.

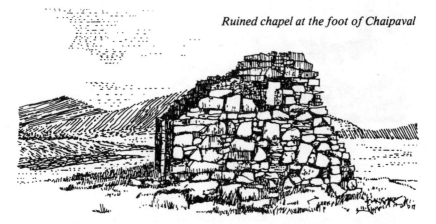

Ruined chapel at the foot of Chaipaval

Stride on to pass through a gate and continue along the clear track in the direction of a ruin on a small eminence. This is Rubh' an Teampuill, thought to have been built in the early 16th century, about the time of St Clement's at Rodel, and visited on Walk 18.

Head on along the track through the machair to a stile in the wall. Beyond, turn right and begin the long, stiff climb towards the summit of Chaipaval, bearing to the right, through a

63

magnificent rockery of heather that continues for a thousand feet. On the flattish top a good path continues through a peaty wasteland, first to the triangulation point and then to the summit cairn. Enjoy the wonderful views in all directions of Harris and the many islands scattered around its skirts.

To return, descend by your outward route, or follow the contours round the north-east side of the hill, dropping steadily through the heather and peaty moorland to a gate in the fence. From here, walk down through the machair to pick up one of several tracks leading right to your car.

Oystercatcher on the machair

Information

Distance: *5½ miles*
Time: *4 hours*
Map: *Landranger 18 reference 968931 (Chaipaval summit)*
Terrain: *Stiff scramble whichever route is taken to the summit.*

18. A Walk from St Clement's Church, Rodel, to Renish Point

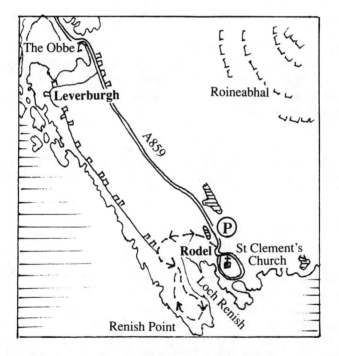

The Obbe

Leverburgh

Roineabhal

A859

Rodel

P

St Clement's Church

Renish Point

Loch Renish

Head south from Tarbert on the A859 and after three miles take the left turn signposted Meavag and Drinishader. Here starts a glorious drive along the single-track road, passing through Plocrapool, Scadabay, Grosebay, Stockinish, Geocrab, Manish, Flodabay, Lingarabay and finally Rodel. The narrow

St Clement's Church, Rodel

road twists and turns, following the deeply-indented coastline. Stretching inland are vast areas of bare rock, scraped clean of any soil by an ancient glacier. Heather and peat bog fill the gaps between the huge rock sheets but on some slopes field gentian grows in large numbers.

Park outside St Clement's Church. It dates from the first decades of the 16th century and, after various vicissitudes, was restored to its present state by the Countess of Dunmore in 1873.

Climb the slope to the church, to see the austere interior and perhaps to climb its sturdy tower. Thought to have been built by the Macleods of Dunvegan, the church was the family's traditional burial place and there are three Macleod tombs. The principal one was constructed in 1528, 20 years before the death of the chief, Alasdair Crotach. The tomb is set in a recessed arch in the south wall, and the tombstone depicts a knight in armour carved in local black gneiss rock. The recess is elaborately carved and shows the 12 apostles, a pair of angels and the Holy Trinity.

Walk round the small churchyard, which is overlooked by the formidable mountains of Mullach na Stughadh and Coire Ròineabhail, their tops veiled in mist. Here in small walled enclosures are the tombs of Macdonalds and Macleods. In several of these flourish the wild fuchsia laden with red flowers.

Drive on a hundred yards and park on a verge in front of a ruined house. Walk along the road to take a reinforced track on the left. It runs beside a picturesque loch where amphibious bistort flowers and fish jump. Cross a wooden bridge over the exit stream that flows into the sea loch, Loch Rodel. Overhead a buzzard flies over the heather slopes, keening eerily as it goes.

Fuchsia

Stride ahead from the bridge to walk a wide grassy track until you reach a fence, then follow it right and climb the flower-bedecked cliff overlooking Loch Rodel. From here there is a good view over the islands in the Sound of Harris. Pass through the gate and continue along the pleasing path. The way drops down and then swings left and climbs to another gate.

Press on further and cross an access track to a house, and then on to reach a metalled road. Twenty yards on, turn left down a very narrow road, where tansy flowers, to its end at the head of the loch. Pass through a gate on the right and walk up onto the headland. Follow the fence, keeping to the right of it, as it climbs steadily upwards. On reaching a boundary fence ahead of you, bear right to a gate. Beyond, look for the cairn on the highest point and cross over the pathless moorland, picking the easiest and the driest route to it. As you go, notice the fine lazy-beds that start on the drier ground and continue, sloping downwards, into a much wetter area.

When you reach the cairn, sit and enjoy the spectacular view. Over to the east lie the Shiant Islands and, beyond, the mountains of the mainland. Look south-east to see the mountains of Skye. Due south, across the Sound of Harris, you can see the hills that form the spine of the Uists. To the south-west lie the islands of Killegray and Ensay, both uninhabited but with excellent grazing for sheep and cattle. Beyond these lies Berneray, the only inhabited island in the Sound of Harris.

Beyond the cairn the moorland slopes down to Renish Point. Look for curious seals in the waters around the rocks and gannets flying fast over the sea. Eider ducks coo quietly from close inshore and oystercatchers and a curlew call from a rocky fang projecting from the sea.

Retrace your outward route to rejoin your car. To return to Tarbert, continue along the A859. Visit Leverburgh, formerly Obbe. It was renamed by Lord Leverhulme in 1923 when he tried to transform the township into a fishing port. When he died in 1925 the project was abandoned and many of the port buildings were dismantled. Further on, pass the glorious sands of Northton, Seilebost and Luskentyre. This return route provides a delightful contrast to that taken on your outward journey along the east coast.

Information

Distance: 4½ miles
Time: 2-3 hours
Map: Landranger 18 reference 048832 (St Clement's Church)
Terrain: Easy walking most of the way. May be wet over the Point. Choose the best way over the heather moorland.

19. A Circular Walk from Kendebig, near Tarbert

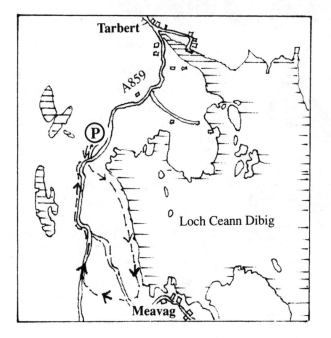

Leave Tarbert by the A859 and drive south steadily, climbing for two miles. Park in an old road on the right side of the hill. Open the small green gate on the opposite side of the road and walk down the lovely grassy path that continues beside an inlet of Loch Ceann Dibig, passing a crofthouse on your right. Look for seals sitting on the rocks and oystercatchers feeding on the seaweed. Wheatears flit about the rocks. A cormorant

Loch Ceann Dibig

catches a small dab and consumes it whole, after dropping it once on finding the width of the fish difficult to manage. Afterwards its throat bulges as the fish passes lower and lower.

Pass by a ruined blackhouse. From the glorious path there are delightful views of the islands of Scotasay and Scalpay. The path winds below steep cliffs, with heather and willow growing on the ledges. Once through a further gate, stroll over tormentil scattered among the sphagnum. Follow the path as it continues behind two cottages and then passes over a small bridge.

Wheatears flit about the rocks

Stride the pretty path beside the island-girt sea loch. Close to the shore rowan trees laden with red berries attract several thrushes. The path then climbs a hill where lousewort and spearwort flower. Further on a small lochan lies to the right. Walk on and through a gate by a larger loch where bogbean and cotton-grass grow and hoodies scold from a rocky outcrop.

The path comes beside another crofthouse where a vast clump of iris grows with gipsywort flowering among the green spear-like leaves. Follow the access track to the road. Turn left and just after the next house look for a gate on the right. Pass through and walk the slope to the next gate. Beyond, continue ahead to a small loch and cross the bridge over a hurrying stream.

Take a narrow path from the bridge that heads right (west), and stroll on in this direction after it peters out. Keep climbing steadily, until you reach a much bigger loch, set amid heather and rocky outcrops and covered in parts with water lilies and water lobelia.

Bear right, to round the end of the loch, and walk the clear track uphill that passes close to a tumbling burn. The track leads between peat cuttings and comes to the A859. Turn right along the moorland road, past several more lochs. From here you can see the dramatic Shiant Islands and a long stretch of mountains on the mainland. Ahead, about Tarbert, lie the hills of Harris, more bare rock than grassy slopes where glaciers of long ago carried away the soil. Continue along the road to rejoin your car.

Information

Distance: 3 miles
Time: 1½ hours
Map: Landranger 14 reference 145982 (lay-by)
Terrain: Generally easy, wet in places. Can be rough walking where
*   the path ceases between the two lochs.*

20. A Walk to the Lighthouse, Eilean Glas, on the Isle of Scalpay

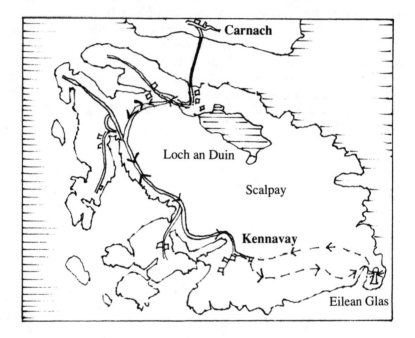

Scalpay lies in the mouth of East Loch Tarbert. Until recently it was a disconnected island reached by a small ferry operated by the Western Isles Council. This has now been displaced by a new causeway which carries the road across the sound, about a quarter of a mile to the west of the old ferry crossing.

This walk was originally planned to start from the ferry terminal. If you now drive across the causeway, you should look out for a suitable off-road parking place before you reach the main village, to enable you to enjoy the island's atmosphere on foot.

Follow the road down towards the south harbour, cross the bridge and go up the other side past the school and community centre. You will see the Scotland Free Church high on the hill on the left. Wherever you walk, the air resounds with the calls of gulls. Young blackbacks plead to be fed and harass their parents when they gain no response.

Carry on past the Church of Scotland. Notice the solid well-kept houses of the island. Scalpay has a prosperous and vigorous community for whom the sea has always provided a livelihood. Several fishing vessels operate from the island, catching scallops and prawns. And there is an

Hardhead and scabious

increasing number of smaller boats that are used to fish for prawns, crabs and lobsters round the coasts of Harris and Skye.

After two miles, climb a steepish hill, turn left and follow the road to a gate that has an arrow and a notice saying 'To the lighthouse'. Continue ahead through another gate, generally open. Beyond, look right to see a narrow stile that gives access to a shallow valley between two long outcrops of gneiss.

Walk along this short valley and look for a red disk on a telegraph pole. Red disks, placed on shoulder-height posts or on telegraph posts, direct you safely over the moorland. The way lies to the left after the first valley, it then heads seawards, before heading left again. This change of direction is repeated twice to bring you to a gate in a long well-built stone wall. Near the beginning of this moorland walk there is a sizeable wet area but with care you can negotiate it with dry boots.

Lighthouse at Eilean Glas

Pass through the gate and continue towards the next post supporting a red disk. Shortly afterwards the lighthouse comes fully into view. Walk round the excellent small harbour, and then over the isthmus of gneiss towards the red and white lighthouse with its large red foghorn.

One of the first lighthouses to be built in Scotland was constructed on this promontory in 1788. The present tower was built between 1824 and 1826. It was designed by Robert Stevenson, the grandfather of Robert Louis Stevenson. The light is now automatic and its rays beam out over the Minch. Below the tower is a house which was occupied in 1789 by Alexander Reid, the first keeper, who lived in this remote, lonely outpost for 35 years.

From the lighthouse you can see the Shiant Isles and the mountains of Skye. Overhead a pair of merlin quarter the heathery tops and then suddenly one darts and weaves, dives and pounces on a meadow pipit. Shags fly low over the waves below the cliffs and gannets in groups travel fast towards the Shiants.

To return, head on from the lighthouse, aiming for a red-topped yellow plastic pole. This will lead you to another gate in the same wall, to the right of a small loch. Follow the tall, thin yellow posts across the moorland, this time by a different, but still peaty, route. They lead you to the side of a strongly-fenced small generator and the road. Continue along this until you reach the two gates at the start of the moorland walk.

Return along the narrow road, with good views of the Clisham range ahead, to return to your parking place

Information

Distance: *7 miles*
Time: *3-4 hours*
Map: *Landranger 14 reference 247949 (lighthouse)*
Terrain: *Road walking easy. Moorland walk could be wet.*

21. A Circular Walk to Rhenigidale

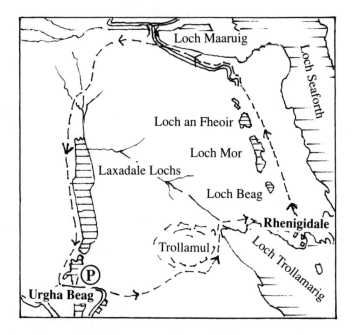

Leave Tarbert by the road to Kyles Scalpay. Park in a largish lay-by just beyond the bridge across the Laxadale Lochs (grid reference 184005). The footpath is signposted Rhenigidale. Follow the clear, reinforced, grassy path that climbs steadily upwards through heather moorland. Look for oak eggar moth caterpillars, making seemingly perilous crossings of the path. Several small burns bisect the path and you can cross these on footbridges.

As you climb, look left for your first sighting of Clisham. Look back to see Kendebig, part of the area traversed in Walk 19. Continue until you reach a cairn from where there is a dramatic view of the Sound of Shiant with the islands beyond. Below lies the sea loch, Trollamarig. Walk on, descending the zig-zagging path as it makes short tight bends down the very steep side of Trollamul to the loch. To the left you can just glimpse the lovely waterfalls that plummet down the steep-sided Glen Trollamarig.

Rowan and berries

Cross the bridge over the burn, which hurries to empty its water into the sheltered bay. Then begin to ascend the easier zig-zags that climb up the cliffs ahead. Great whalebacks of gneiss, riven and scratched during glaciation, stand on either side of the path. Pass through several derelict blackhouses. A pretty fall foams between two of the houses. Head on along the path, past a small ravine where rowan and willow thrive, through a gate, and on to the junction with the new road. Until this was built in 1989 there was no road to Rhenigidale. It could be approached either by boat or by the footpath you have taken.

Turn right and walk into the settlement. Its six or seven houses — one of which is a youth hostel — nestle around its tiny bay.

Return along the road, climbing steadily through the moonscape hills. Stride past Loch Beag, Loch Mór and Loch an Fheòir. Suddenly the road begins to descend and Loch Seaforth with its island comes into view. Follow the road as it swings left beside Loch Maaruig. Walk to the head of the loch, where a heron rises and flies off into Loch Seaforth. As you approach the bridge over the Maaruig River, look for a gate on the left of the road. Pass through and walk the track, signposted 'Path to Tarbert', beyond.

Carry on where the track swings left and passes over very wet moorland. Away to the right the top of Clisham is veiled in mist. The path climbs steadily to a cairn. Beyond and below is a good view of Laxadale Lochs with the track running along the right bank. Follow the track until you reach the road. Turn left and walk down the slope to rejoin your car.

Laxadale Lochs

Information

Distance: 11 miles
Time: 4-5 hours
Map: Landranger 14 reference 184005 (car parking)
Terrain: A good path all the way to the new road. The track to the Tarbert Road is wet in places and requires some boulder-hopping.

22. A Circular Walk on the Island of Berneray

Leave Lochmaddy by the A865 and head north-west for five miles before turning right onto the B893. This road used to branch to the right at Port-Nan-Long to the Berneray car ferry, but the boat has been displaced by a new causeway, which sweeps the road across the sound and joins the island a short distance to the west of the old slipway. If you now drive across the causeway, you should look out for a suitable off-road parking spot soon afterwards, to enable you to enjoy the feel of the island on foot.

Follow the road to the T-junction, where it bears to the right down to the little harbour of Poll an Oir. Stride on to pass the jetty at Loch a Bhaigh, where the passenger ferry to Harris calls on request. The jetty and harbour buildings were erected in 1988 and are also owned by the Island's Council. Continue round Bays Loch. Notice the shop on the left because this is where you will turn off the road later for your walk along the sands. Carry on walking towards the school, which you reach by taking the right fork, where the road divides.

Just before the school, at Ruisgarry, look right to see several blackhouses. These were occupied until the late 1970s when the people were rehoused. Much of the old furniture is still to be seen but the weather will soon destroy this fascinating reminder of the past. Walk on round the headland towards the youth hostel where several blackhouses have been carefully restored to accommodate 14 visitors.

Blackhouses restored for hostels

You may wish to continue along the narrow coast road to view the ruins of a church on your left, on a hill. This was built by the 19th-century engineer Thomas Telford and used by the people of Berneray and of the Island of Pabbay. Return along the coast road, past the shop noted earlier, and take a narrow road, signposted Brusda, on the right. The road climbs gently through the green fields and then drops steadily down. Where it swings sharply left, continue ahead along a reinforced track, keeping to the right of a crofthouse. Beyond a gate the track leads, still reinforced, to another gate which you pass through.

Beyond, a wide grassy track winds over the magnificent machair, where green plovers, curlews, oystercatchers and snipe enjoy the pastures. Pass through a gate into the dunes and follow the way through walls of

Seaweeds from the beach

sand and marram, some 20 to 30 feet in height, to walk down onto the splendid west beach. Turn left to stroll the shell-sand, which has a scattering of many species of seaweed. Here a flock of ringed plover run through the weed after a multitude of sand flies, brought out by the afternoon sun.

Over the turquoise and then purple water you can see Pabbay. From this island people rowed over to the ruined church seen earlier, called by a great bell that sounded for miles. Below the heather-covered high ground lie green pastures and one dwelling house.

Walk for two-and-a-half miles along the glorious sands, where the surf breaks gently. The next green island you see is Boreray. Leave the great strand of sand just where the low cliffs begin, to pick up one of several grassy tracks winding through the sand dunes and then over the machair. The track passes below the ruins of a herdsman's hut on the Knoll of Skulls. The mound is supposed to be partly composed of the skulls of miscreants.

Pass through the gate and turn left to walk through the machair on a reinforced track. This brings you to the community centre, built in 1985, where you might be tempted to try its delicious snacks. Walk up the road from the centre to pass through the township of Borve. At the T-junction, turn right to return to your parking place.

Information

Distance: 9½ miles
Time: 6 hours
Map: Landranger 18 reference 917799 (jetty)
Terrain: Easy walking all the way.

23. A Circular Walk on the Island of Berneray

As described in the previous section, the Island of Berneray has now been joined to North Uist by a causeway. You can take advantage of this and drive onto the island, and find yourself an unobtrusive parking spot soon after you have crossed the water.

From your parking spot walk ahead, following the road, which is bordered with a variety of wild flowers. Continue as it swings right, with a grand view of the mountains of Harris ahead. Stride past the Lobster Pot tea room, leaving the pleasure of good snacks and tea until the end of the day. Carry on round the side of a small creek, Poll an Oir. It is used as a temporary harbour, with brightly-painted boats pulled up out of the water.

Turn left to walk through Borve, a village built in 1900. The last house on the left is Donald Mackillop's, where Prince Charles stayed on a crofting holiday. Continue downhill towards the community centre where various activities take place, including Berneray Week. The centre provides snacks and teas, but is closed on Sunday and Monday.

Walk in front of the centre and pass through a gate on its right, which has a notice asking you to shut the gate. Strike ahead, bearing slightly left, towards a number of boulders. Look for two that are shaped like seats. These chairstones are believed to date from Viking times and were used during the settling of disputes.

Return to the centre and follow the reinforced track that continues. Here a merlin tries to fly down a meadow pipit. The raptor twists and turns after its victim and rises to swoop but is disturbed from its kill by a flock of green plover, which mob it incessantly until it flies off.

Head along the track as it passes out onto the machair, where rye and barley grow. Among these crops are masses of buttercups, corn marigolds, red poppies and charlock. Continue where the machair has been left fallow and here the ground is covered with summer flowers. Look for field gentians, yellow pansies, mauve and kidney vetch, hayrattle, pink and white clover, eyebright, daisies and buttercups.

Green plovers

Where the track swings left, pass through a gate on the right and make for the top of the small hill. From here look north over the vast stretch of machair. On the top is a small hut, now a ruin, but once used by a herdsman whose job was to keep the cattle out of the crops. From this hill you can walk to the glorious sands beyond the dunes.

Now bear east towards a tall man-made cairn, which is surrounded by a small wall and odd stones. The cairn was erected in 1991 to commemorate Angus MacAskill, who lived almost 130 years ago. Angus, a giant 7 feet 9 inches in height, was born in a croft on the site of the cairn. He left Berneray when he was six, emigrating with his family to Nova Scotia. He was reputed to be the strongest man in the world. The *Guinness Book of Records* states that Angus was a non-pathological, or true, giant. The cairn has been built 7 feet 9 inches high.

Continue along the edge of the Sound, heading towards a walled burial ground. Most of the cemeteries in the Western Isles are built on a slope, facing the sea. The majority are found on the west coast; on the east there is not enough soil for burial.

Walk along the low headland until the sea loch, Loch Borve, comes into view. This wide stretch of water has pleasing sandy margins and at low tide the water recedes completely, exposing an entire sandy bed. As you near the loch, join a grassy track that runs beside it. Cross a small stone bridge over an access stream and then press ahead across the machair to join the reinforced track that leads to the community centre.

Continue along the road taken earlier, through Borve, and turn right at the end of the road. Carry on until you are a few yards beyond the tea room. From here, strike right up the hill, Beinn A' Chlaidh, to a cairn. Then walk ahead to a large stone which stands 8 feet high with another 8 feet below ground. Once it was encircled with three rings of boulders, but these have long been removed and used for building the walls, houses and dykes of Borve.

From the stone, return by the same route to the road, either to obtain refreshments or make your way straight back to your car.

Standing stone on Beinn A' Chlaidh

Information

Distance: 5 miles
Time: 3 hours
Map: Landranger 18 reference 917799 (jetty)
Terrain: Easy walking all the way. Could be wet underfoot on the hill with the standing stone.

24. A Circular Walk to Ben Scolpaig

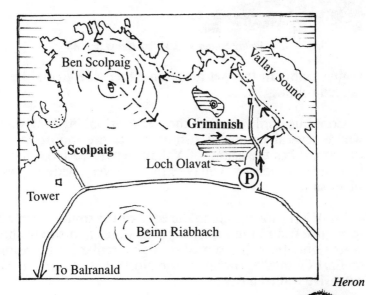

Heron

From Lochmaddy, take the A865 north west as it skirts the coast, and turn off at the narrow road leading to Loch Olavat (grid reference 752750). Park on the turf beyond a large unmarked passing area. Look for a merlin flying low over the heather, prospecting for prey. Ahead lies the loch, where a heron fishes and a pair of swans marshal their cygnets. Cross the cattle grid and, just before the causeway, follow the narrow road that

Vallay Sound with Vallay Island beyond

swings right. In the wet areas on either side grows the pretty ragged robin.

Continue until you reach the pier overlooking Vallay Sound, where several colourful fishing boats are moored. Beyond the sound lies the island of Vallay, separated from the mainland at low tide by Vallay Strand, a very wide expanse of silver sand.

Walk left (north), along the edge of the sound, with a fence to your left and the gently lapping water and sandy shore to your right. Pass in front of a large circular house belonging to Earl Granville, owner of the North Uist estates. It has an extensive walled garden.

Stroll along the sandy turf, which is alive with rabbits and starlings — perhaps the most common bird to be seen in the Western Isles. Continue ahead past several glorious bays white with shell sand. At the fence, either walk right and clamber over easily-negotiated rocks or walk left to a gate in the fence. Look for small flocks of ringed plover hurrying over the wet sand left by the receding tide.

The next bay is full of jagged rocks, thrusting into the sea. Great cobalt-blue rollers come roaring in and break on the rocks with huge fountains of white foam. Here rock pipits flit about the boulders and sea thrift grows on the turf. Keep to the right of the fence and follow it to the end, where again you need to scramble over rocks.

Walk ahead over large clumps of heather, whose scent fills the air. Young and adult shags sit in a long row on a jagged ridge of rock close to the crashing waves. All is desolate and magnificent. Proceed with care to a large hole in the green turf. Peer over to see large bubbles of foam covering the floor of a deep cavern created when the roof collapsed. Walk round the gaping hole and move over to the cliff face, again with great care, to see the foam of the waves being thrust through an arch in the cliff, connecting with the cavern. On the ledges of the cliff fulmars nest and large downy young flex their wings and attempt to fly.

Head on along the cliffs until you can see the lovely sands of Scolpaig, with the Scolpaig farm behind. At this point you can also see Scolpaig Tower, the Western Isles' only folly. It was constructed in the last century, during a famine relief scheme, from the remains of a dun. Strike left up the heathery slopes of Ben Scolpaig, crossing two small hills, before attaining the triangulation point at 300 feet. Pause here to enjoy the extensive view. Beyond Haskeir Island, you can just discern St Kilda.

From the hilltop you can also see your car parked beyond Loch Olavat. Drop down the slope towards it, aiming for a gate in the fence behind a ruined hut. Suddenly from close to the hut 15 large red stags appear and peer curiously before bounding over the fence with great ease and hurrying up the land beyond the lake towards Beinn Riabhach.

Once through the gate continue ahead, bearing slightly left to avoid a wettish area. From the loch on the right comes a clonking clamour of dozens of grey lag-geese, cropping the grass. They rise and fly off in ordered lines, ackh-ackhing as they go.

On reaching the boundary wall, walk left to a gate in a fence. Stride ahead along the short stony track and then turn right along the causeway over the end of Loch Olavat. Press ahead to rejoin your car.

Before leaving this area, you might wish to head south along the A865 to the turn-off to Hougharry. This leads to Balranald, a Royal Society for the Protection of Birds reserve where you can see many species and some splendid machair. There is a resident warden in the summer months.

Information

Distance: *5 miles*
Time: *3-4 hours*
Map: *Landranger 18 reference 752750 (Loch Olavat)*
Terrain: *Generally easy walking. Heathery slopes and wet areas on Ben Scolpaig require care.*

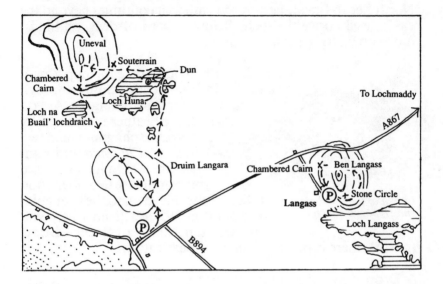

25. A Short Circular Walk to see a Stone Circle and a Chambered Cairn on Ben Langass

Leave Lochmaddy by the A867 and take the well-signposted track to Langass Hotel and to the stone circle. Park in front of the hotel and walk on along the continuing track. Just before the end, take a footpath leading left up the slope through heather and bracken. Below lies Loch Langass, a long stretch of sparkling water.

The path soon brings you to the oval-shaped stone circle, known as Pobull Thinn (Fingal's People), where some of the stones are still upright. It stands on a platform cut into the hillside. Stand in the circle and enjoy the grand view of the lochs and islands of North Uist and of the small range of hills, from North Lee to Eaval. Follow the path as it continues beyond the circle, well above the loch. Below, a herd of deer, all hinds, move down to the water to drink.

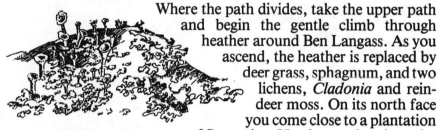

Where the path divides, take the upper path and begin the gentle climb through heather around Ben Langass. As you ascend, the heather is replaced by deer grass, sphagnum, and two lichens, *Cladonia* and reindeer moss. On its north face you come close to a plantation

Lichen of the Cladonia and Hypogymnia types

of Scots pine. Head on to the triangulation point at 295 feet from where you can see a necklace of lochs. Below (north), there is much evidence of peat cutting.

Drop down the slope towards a great mound of stones. This is a neolithic chambered cairn, Bharpa Langais, with a charming skirt of heather and various ferns. Beyond a small entrance and two stone lintels is a burial chamber. It was used first in the second or third millenium B.C., and later in the early Bronze Age.

Chambered cairn on Ben Langass

From the cairn strike diagonally left (south-east) and walk over the moorland to rejoin the track, which leads to your car.

Information

Distance: 2 miles
Time: 1-2 hours
Map: Landranger 18 reference 843654 (Ben Langass)
Terrain: Moorland walking — can be hard walking over heather,
          but beautiful to look at.

26. A Circular Walk to see a Prehistoric Underground House and an Impressive Standing Stone

Leave Lochmaddy by the A867 and once past the B894 turn-off for Sidinish, park in a large lay-by on the right. Walk back a few yards and turn left into a track opposite the B894. Continue past an old quarry and walk down the track. It comes beside a fenced area on the right where the soil has been reseeded after improvement with fertiliser and has attracted a flock of curlew. Where the track branches, take the right fork to walk a short peaty track out onto heather moorland. Ahead stands the hill Uneval (460 feet), and its antiquities, the aim of the walk.

Where the fence swings away to the right, bear diagonally right to cross a plateau, called the Druim Langara. Several great skuas fly overhead. Gradually descend from the plateau, traversing the boggy moorland with care, keeping to the right of a small lochan and right also of the much larger Loch Huna. Continue ahead between Loch Huna and another lochan to your right. To make sure you are heading in the right direction, look for the very green patch on the right slope (east) of Uneval.

The small lochan on your right receives water from Loch Huna and this outlet stream needs to be crossed at the narrowest point. The best place is just before it joins the small sheet of water where white water lilies grow. Walk back along the side of the stream, enjoying the yellow water lilies and bur-reed.

A wren scolds from a heather
stalk. Then continue around
Loch Huna, following the
deer tracks for the easiest
way. Look for grouse, deer
droppings and otter spraints.

Wren

Climb the slope to the green patch
to see the remains of an under-
ground house (souterrain on the O.S.
map). From this green grassy area,
encircled by peaty moorland, you can see
the large cairn visited on Walk 25. Look
down to Loch Huna to see an island with a
pile of stones on it and a row, like a causeway,
almost joining the island to the shore. This is one of many duns,
or forts, found in lochs in the Western Isles.

Here a decision has to be made, either to follow the contours
west round Uneval to visit the chambered cairn and standing
stone or to climb to the flattish and very wet top of the hill.
The splendid view from the summit, of innumerable inland
lochs, sea lochs, extensive moorland and the hills of North Uist,
makes the climb worthwhile, but take care crossing those high
peat hags. From the summit, descend south to view the large
standing stone and the remains of a chambered cairn and an
ancient house. What magnificent sites these prehistoric people
chose — they could see for miles.

Chambered cairn on Uneval

From the standing stone, look down to see the gate through the fence, half a mile across the moor. To reach this, drop down the slope and walk the wet area between Loch na Buail 'lochdraich and Loch Huna. Beyond the gate walk diagonally left to a gate close to Loch Huna, where white and yellow water lilies grow together. Once through the second gate, climb Druim Langara (half a mile), still heading slightly left. Continue until the fenced area of grassland comes into view. Beside it is the peaty track, which soon joins the track to the road.

Information

Distance: *5½ miles*
Time: *3 hours*
Map: *Landranger 18 reference 809674 (souterrain)*
Terrain: *A moorland walk that can be wet underfoot for most of the way. Map reading required.*

27. A Walk over Moorland, by a glorious Loch, and a Climb up North Uist's highest Mountain

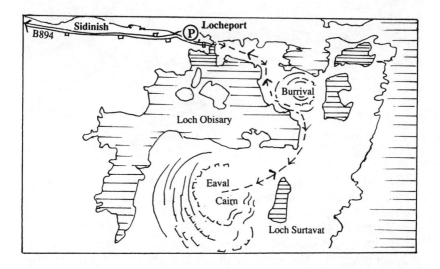

Leave Lochmaddy by the A867 and after seven miles take the B894, signposted Locheport and Sidinish. This B road runs along a small ridge above the sea loch, Loch Eport, which lies to the left. Continue to the end of the road where there is a good parking area and a dramatic view of Eaval (1138 feet), the main aim of the walk.

Pass through a small gate beyond the parking space and head on, passing to the right of a crofthouse. Follow the track as it curves right and then left to pass through an open gate. Out on the sea loch a fisherman stands in his boat leisurely setting his nets. Follow the fence posts over the moor to pass a small bay with a small sturdy wall of stones, creating a little harbour. Climb the heathery path and continue across a wet area to walk past another small bay from where a heron flies off across Loch Eport. The track leads to a substantial bank of stones across the outflow stream from the freshwater Loch Obisary. The tide comes in on the left of the stones and its water flows into Loch Obisary. Look for patches of seaweed on the freshwater side.

Track and stepping stones

Cross the stepping stones and walk out onto the moor, taking a path through the softly-scented heather. Follow it as it swings right and keeps above a very wet area, full of large pools. Ahead lies Burrival (460 feet), a solid, round-topped small mountain where ravens congregate. Press on along an often indistinct way, aiming for the gate in the fence ahead, slightly to the right of the centre of Burrival. From over the top of the small mountain an eagle glides effortlessly. Soon it attracts the attention of a pair of geese, which honk loudly as they mob it relentlessly until it moves away.

Once beyond the gate you have a choice, either to climb Burrival and enjoy its sunny rocky slopes or to continue towards the formidable-looking Eaval, which now lies to your right across Loch Obisary. To reach Eaval, turn right and begin the delightful walk below Burrival over clear tracks made by deer, sheep and humans along the heathery slopes of Loch Obisary's many small bays. High on the slopes a merlin flies over the heather and then dives out of sight. The loch, an artist's paradise, has many small islands, all lush with vegetation that is out of reach of the voracious sheep.

Look for stonechats sitting on bracken stalks; their families are now airborne and these small brown birds seem to be everywhere. Cross the fence that lies flat on the ground at the head of the loch and continue. When you reach the narrow but deep outflow stream from Loch Surtavat hurrying to reach Loch Obisary, walk upstream to find an easy place to cross.

Then begin the gradual ascent of the north-east slopes of Eaval. These are a glorious mix of long outcrops of gneiss, giving a good grip for walking boots, and long hollows of grass and heather sloping upwards between the rock. As you climb, more and more familiar islands, hills, lochs and peaks come into view. And then suddenly you are on the summit, where stands a triangulation point set in a cairn enclosed within a stone shelter. The view is quite perfect.

Ravens on Eaval

To the north, you can see the mountains of North Harris and the Lewis coast beyond. Nearer you can see Chaipaval, Hushinish and Berneray. And then to the west lie the magnificent sands of North Uist and the islands of Baleshare and Kirkibost. Out to sea beyond the Monach Islands you can discern St Kilda and Boreray. South and below lies Benbecula, with more water than land, the latter linked with seemingly tiny strings, the causeways. It looks as if the next gale could blow the land out to sea. Beyond lie the mountains of South Uist. To the east the

Kintyre mountains are visible. Nearer, on Skye, you can see the Tables of Macleod, Loch Dunvegan, Vaternish Point, Quiraing, Loch Bracadale and the Fiskavaig cliffs and, over all, the Cuillin peaks, seeming to pierce the clouds. And as you swing round to Harris once more, the Shiants come into view.

All round the mountain lie many lochs, fitting together as neatly as a jig-saw. Leave the summit by the route taken to ascend, aiming for the sandy shores of small bays at the head of Loch Obisary. Return by the same route.

Information

Distance: 9½-10 miles
Time: 5-6 hours
Map: Landrangers 18 and 22 reference 899607 (summit of Eaval)
Terrain: The moorland is wet underfoot. The ascent presents no problems for experienced hill walkers. Find out from the North Uist Estates if you will interfere with the deer calving or stalking before you go.

28. A Short Circular Walk from Lochmaddy

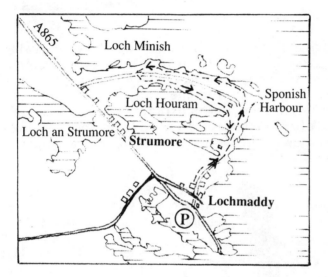

Park as close as convenient to the Old Courthouse (built 1827) in Lochmaddy. Follow the sign for the Uist Outdoor Centre, passing the police station. A host of young pied wagtails flit about the surface of the narrow road, where marsh woundwort grows in the ditches on either side. Pass the outdoor centre on the left and a big stack of peat on the right. Ahead is a grand view of many small green islands with skirts of brown seaweed and, between, the bright blue water of the sea.

Look left to see Chaipaval and Toe Head (see Walk 17) and ahead the wonderful range of mountains that is the island of Harris. The track winds round a bay of the sea loch. Pass

101

Suspension bridge near Lochmaddy

through a kissing-gate and follow the track as it swings right and then left. Two large herons island-hop. Continue to a splendid suspension bridge, built by the army, over an inlet of the sea. Look down from the bridge to see a large underwater garden of oar weed, its fronds dragged out by the tide. Walk the catwalk beyond the bridge and on to an open gate to Sponish House, now a ruin. Do not pass through but bear right, keeping to the right of a fence.

Cormorant

At the corner of the fence, strike right across rough pasture to the edge of the shore, and walk on to the left of a large grey shed standing by the pier at Sponish Harbour. A large cormorant, with mouth agape, flies out into Loch Maddy. Leave the pier and then strike right along the shoreline, bordering Loch Minish. This is a lovely corner of North Uist, with dozens of small islands floating in a blue-blue sea.

Continue to the narrow road and turn left. Ahead of you as you walk you can see the rocky slopes of North Lee, South Lee, Burrival and Eaval, all of which shelter Lochmaddy from the winds from the east. On the right stretches the freshwater Loch Houram. Walk to the grey building by the pier and turn right to retrace your steps to your car.

Information

Distance:	4½ miles
Time:	2 hours
Map:	Landranger 18 reference 922694 (suspension bridge)
Terrain:	Easy walking all the way.

29. A Linear Walk to cross a Causeway onto an Island to view Seals

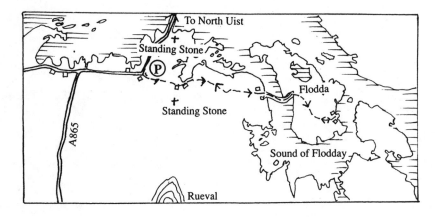

To view the seals on Flodda, park in an open area beside the A865. If travelling from the north, cross the causeway that unites North Uist with Benbecula. Look for the first road junction on the left, and park on the corner. The grid reference is 820557. Walk along the narrow lane where willow and irises grow. Pass a small loch with large banks of heather and watch a brown duck swim with its last duckling. Stride along a small causeway across another loch where white water lilies grow. Water mint flowers among more willow.

To the left is a good view of Eaval. Just before a wooden bridge over an inlet of the sea, look for two gate stoops with a

Standing stone with Eaval in background

low wire fence between. Step over this and follow the indistinct path through the heather to another gate, diagonally right. Beyond, continue to a standing stone, proud among a small circle of stones. From this small eminence there is a pleasing view of the hills and the many areas of water, both fresh and salt, sparkling and gleaming in the sunlight. Away to the east, the mountains of Skye stand out with startling clarity in the wonderfully clear light. A flock of curlews rise as one and fly off over the moorland.

Return to the road and look for the old stone house with a turf roof just before the wooden bridge, which you cross. Carry on where young rock pipits flit about the wire fences and then follow the road as it moves out onto open moorland. Head on past another inland loch to a causeway over the Sound of Flodday onto the island of Flodda.

Continue along the narrow lane until you reach a broken gate that once gave access to a track to a modern house. Do not take the track but turn right and pass through another gate to walk a grassy path. It leads towards a crofthouse where you turn right to follow a sheep trod through bracken up onto a small hillock.

From here there is a delightful view of the many islands in the sound between North Uist and Benbecula. On several of these, dozens of grey seals snooze or laze. Some swim, surface and then struggle onto the shore. Nearby on its look-out, a

Snoozing grey seals

rocky outcrop, a merlin watches for prey. Then it rises swiftly on its long narrow wings before striking downwards on its victim.

Return from this glorious vantage point and walk back the same way as taken on your outward journey. If there is a shower, you may be lucky to see some magnificent rainbows.

Information

Distance: *4½ miles*
Time: *2-3 hours*
Map: *Landranger 22 reference 820557 (parking)*
Terrain: *Easy walking all the way.*

30. A Linear Walk to Rossinish, Benbecula

Drive south along the A865 over the causeway that connects North Uist with Benbecula. After two-and-a-half miles, turn left and continue for half a mile to park on the left just after an industrial site. Take the continuing reinforced track that runs beside and to the left of the track leading to a gravel pit on the right.

The easy-to-walk track moves out into moorland, where the pungent smelling bog myrtle, now with small yellow catkins, grows among the sweetly-scented heather. It fills the air with its perfume and delights a myriad of bees, flies and red admiral butterflies. Pass the peat cuttings and walk beside Loch Bà Una, where noisy black-backed gulls up-end into the shallow water after prey.

To the left of the track stands Rueval (409 feet), which is covered with heather and has several craggy overhanging outcrops below the top. Under one of these, on the south-east slope and well-hidden by heather, Bonnie Prince Charlie lay hidden for two days. He and his companions, in June 1746, were waiting for Flora Macdonald to arrange their escape.

If you wish to climb the hill, it is easy to reach the triangulation point and the two cairns from the track. The view is spectacular and well worth the effort. A buzzard is chased away from quartering Rueval's slopes by a trio of acrobatic ravens.

Continue past Loch Hermidale on the right, and then Loch na Deighe fo Dheas. There are good views of Eaval, climbed on Walk 27. Cross a small turf causeway between Loch na Deighe fo Thuath and Loch na Deighe fo Dheas and on along the gated track. Where the track divides, take the left fork. Ahead are good views of Skye. Pass the head of Loch an Tairbh and look for the shieling away to the left on a little hill beyond a gate. To the right is a sheep fank, an enclosure where sheep are gathered.

Away to the right the tops of Heckla and Beinn Mhor in South Uist are veiled in soft mist. Press on along the grassy track. To the left lies Flodda (see Walk 29), and beyond its headland you can see the many seals on the small islands in the Sound of Flodday. The next stretch of water on your left is tidal and is an inlet from Flodday Sound. The track continues but it is almost obscured by heather, with clumps of white among the pink. To the right across a loch stands a ruined crofthouse.

Ruined crofthouse

Stride the track as it crosses another grassy cause-way, with salt water to the right and fresh to the left. The way leads through more heather gardens, with a loch to your left where honeysuckle hangs over the water and blackberries are in flower and in fruit. Now the track becomes a narrow path on a small cliff above the loch. To the right, on an inlet of the sea, a rowan laden with berries and an aspen cling to a low cliff face.

Then you come to the last gate and you need to make a decision. Perhaps this is as far as you wish to walk, and you can sit by one of the inlets of the sea looking at the many islands.

Blackberry

If, however, you wish to reach Rossinish, a deserted croft-house, you need to be able to map-read because there are no paths. There is a small path to a small beach but from then on it is best to follow the sheep-tracks in an easterly direction across some rather wet moorland to the side of the largest of three inland lochs. Walk round the north end and then continue ahead to the crofthouse.

When you arrive, be prepared for a surprise. The peaty moorland suddenly becomes sandy and the house is dwarfed by towering sand dunes. In front of the ruin is a grassy sward and below a delightful sandy creek. Bonnie Prince Charlie left here by boat, dressed as a serving maid, for Skye.

Return by the same route.

Information

Distance: *9 miles*
Time: *5-6 hours*
Map: *Landranger 22 reference 811535 (parking)*
Terrain: *Easy walking on the track. Wet moorland from the last gate to Rossinish.*

31. A Short Walk to Old Chapels, a Burial Ground and Thatched Houses

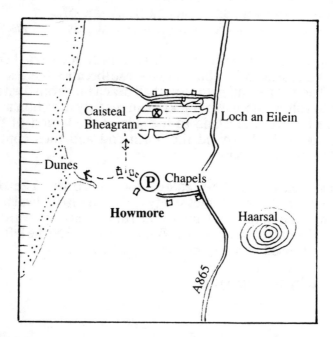

Leave the A865 at the signposted turn-off for Howmore. Drive for half a mile to park in front of the austere church, which has a central communion pew — one of only two in Scotland. Walk across the grass to see the youth hostel, a thatched blackhouse that has been pleasingly restored.

Howmore buildings

Continue across the grass to see the many gravestones in the ancient walled burial ground. This was the graveyard of the Clan Ranald chiefs (see Walk 32). Several pieces of ecclesiastical masonry, heavily encrusted with usnea and an orange lichen, are all that remains of a 12th- or 13th-century college and monastery, destroyed during the Reformation. It is a wonderfully peaceful place. Stand in the far corner to see the ancient ruins, with the blackhouse behind and a later crofthouse, now disused, close by.

Walk back to the hostel and then to the road. Twenty yards back stand two blackhouses, listed buildings still inhabited,

Ruins of college and monastery

which give you a good idea of what much of South Uist would have been like a hundred years ago.

Return to the church and take a pebbly track that leads onto the machair where a hundred or more greylag geese feed noisily and restlessly. Once you are over a slope, a wonderful sandy bay lies ahead. You may wish to continue your walk there. Or you may first like to turn right (north) off the track and a quarter of a mile down a similar track to see Loch an Eilein and its romantic, ruined castle, Bheagram.

Information

Distance: 1-2 miles
Time: 1 hour
Map: Landranger 22 reference 758362 (Howmore)
Terrain: Easy walking.

32. A Circular Walk from Bornish via Rubha Ardvule and Ormiclate

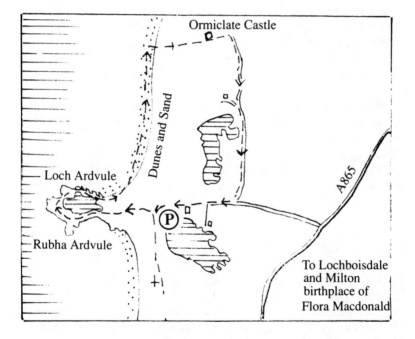

Ormiclate Castle

Dunes and Sand

Loch Ardvule

Rubha Ardvule

A865

P

To Lochboisdale
and Milton
birthplace of
Flora Macdonald

Before starting this walk, you might wish to visit the ruins of the birthplace of Flora Macdonald, which now has a commemorative cairn. A plaque on the cairn tells of her heroism in helping Bonnie Prince Charlie escape to Skye. Drive from Lochboisdale along the A865 for six miles to visit the signposted birthplace at Milton.

Flora Macdonald's cairn

From Milton, drive on for two miles and turn left to Bornish. After less than a mile the road swings right to Ormiclate, but press ahead by the large priest's house on the left and Bornish House on the right. Pass the Catholic church to park on either side of the track, on the machair, after the fencing.

Walk ahead along the track, where cattle graze and a flock of swallows twitter overhead. Regularly, fleetingly, they settle on the tarmac and pick off insects. Beyond the grazing land, stroll beside acres of oats. Here a pale fawn bird with long wings flies into the oats and does not fly out. Is it the elusive corncrake, which spends much of its time in iris beds and rears its young in long grass or in a field of oats?

Stride on along the track where it moves out onto the headland, Rubha Ardvule. Here, to the left, three brightly painted fishing boats shelter in the lee of a curving bay. Halfway along, look for a circular pile of stones, the remnants of Dun Vulan. To the right lies Loch Ardvule, a lovely stretch of water on which a pair of swans rear four cygnets. The outlet of the loch at the tip of the little headland is blocked by a plug of boulders thrown up by the sea.

Where the track ends, cross the spit of boulders and continue round the headland. Look for the stalks of kelp drying in beehive-shaped piles that stand on a bed of boulders. The kelp, washed up in vast quantities, is sold for pharmaceutical purposes.

114

Stacks of kelp, Rubha Ardvule

Pause here for some exciting birdwatching. Flocks of young eider keep close together just offshore. Oystercatchers, ringed plover and dunlin hurry over the sands. A flock of curlews call as they take off as one. Three godwits stand tall between the pied oystercatchers and shags stand and dry their wings.

Head on around the delightful headland and then walk along a narrow path at the base of the dunes. The path eventually leads down to the glorious sandy bay. Stroll along the sands for a mile and a half until you come to a gap in the dunes. From here a grassy track runs inland across the machair towards Ormiclate Castle. If the tide is high, walk the track just behind the narrow line of dunes, passing through two gates to reach the grassy track.

The castle took seven years to build and was completed by the Clan Ranald chief for his French wife in 1708. It burnt down only seven years later, on the eve of the battle of Sherriff Muir where the chief was killed. Today the ruin stands roofless, its stones softened by layers of bright orange lichen.

Walk to the road and turn right. At the T-junction, bear right and make for the Catholic church. Go inside to see the unrendered walls of gneiss and the plain oak pews. All this simplicity acts as a foil to the dramatically-draped altar and colourful robes of the Virgin Mary. It is a lovely church and a splendid way to finish a very good walk. To reach your car, walk down the road to the machair.

On your return, you might care to visit the Kildonan school museum to see an excellent historical exhibition. There is also a very good tea room.

Information

Distance: *6½ miles*
Time: *4 hours*
Map: *Landranger 22 reference 729299 (parking)*
Terrain: *Easy walking all the way.*

33. A Circular Walk to an Ancient Monument, a Wheelhouse, on the Dunes at Kilpheder

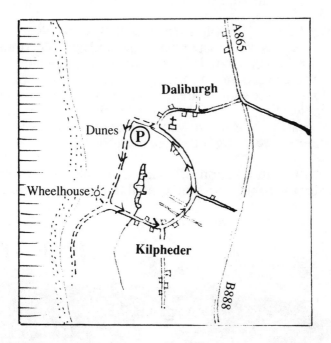

Leave Lochboisdale by the A865. After three miles, turn left onto the B888 at Daliburgh, just before the Borrodale Hotel, then immediately cross over the B road to take a minor road that runs to the side of the hotel. Just beyond the church, turn right and park in a lay-by on the left, opposite sheep-collecting pens and before the fence and gate of the machair.

Beyond the gate, turn left onto the machair to take a sandy track running through alternate areas of oats and fallow land. The latter is covered with a golden glory of buttercups, pansies and ragwort and is the haunt of green plovers. Continue where the track becomes reinforced until you reach a road. Here, turn right to take a track running into the dunes. Thirty yards along, look for two huge dunes to your left. Walk on for a few more yards and then look for the wire fencing that surrounds the wheelhouse.

Marsh or water ragwort

The Kilpheder wheelhouse, or aisled house, is constructed below ground and is periodically filled with blown sand. It is circular with a diameter of ten yards. You can see the entrance passage, which is about eight yards long. In the sunken area, you can see some of the eleven stone spokes that formed chambers. At the centre would have been a hearth. The house was probably roofed with turfs. Wheelhouses are thought to have been Pictish.

Return to the junction of roads and walk ahead towards Kilpheder township, crossing a canal that drains the machair.

Remains of wheelhouse

Ditches along the narrow roadside are lined with water ragwort and irises — a glorious sight in the spring. Keep alert here because you might see an otter. At each road junction turn left and so return to your car, passing bungalows from which comes the pleasing smell of Uist peat being burnt, a more delectable aroma than that emitted by Lewis peat.

On reaching your car, you may wish to continue straight ahead to follow the track that passes through the very tall dunes to a most magnificent beach of shell-sand.

Information

Distance: *2½ miles.*
Time: *1-1½ hours*
Map: *Landranger 31 reference 733203 (wheelhouse)*
Terrain: *Easy walking all the way.*

34. A Walk on the Island of Eriskay

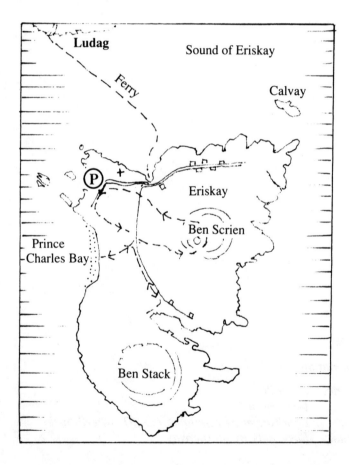

The Eriskay Love Lilt must be on most people's lips as they make their first short ferry trip from Ludag on South Uist to the bewitching island. Eriskay lies between South Uist and Barra, and is surrounded by green and purple seas, the colour caused by the sandy bottom and seaweed drawn out in the currents. The ferry, owned by the Western Isles Council, sails according to suitable tides. It takes a quarter of an hour to cross the Sound of Eriskay and passes small islands on the right where seals bask. To the left lies Calvay Island.

Once on Eriskay, leave the jetty and turn right and then right again, along narrow roads lined with flowers. Climb the hill to see the fine Catholic church of St Michael. Outside, look for the ship's bell recovered from a sunken German battleship. Return to the road and press on, passing the school. At the crossroads keep ahead, dropping down the slope to pass the Politician public house, opened in 1988. This is named after a ship that sank off the island of Calvay in 1941. Among its cargo where 20,000 cases of whisky. Many of these were 'rescued' by the folk of Eriskay and the story has been told in Sir Compton Mackenzie's *Whisky Galore*.

Walk on to pass two burial grounds and continue where the path becomes first a reinforced track and then a grassy track. Look ahead to see the statue of the Madonna on the hillside opposite, placed at the site of an old church. Follow the track right, through harebells and then walk to the left of the football pitch. Climb the slope ahead, which is bordered with field gentians, to reach the road, where you turn right.

Stride ahead along the narrow road above the shore of the luminous green sea. After the top of the hill, take the gate on the right in the fence, opposite the first house on the left as you begin to drop down. Descend the steepish grassy slope. Masses of primroses grow between rocky outcrops. A gate in the right corner of the fance gives access to narrow dunes and the sands. Enjoy this glorious stretch of shell-sand, called Prince Charlie's Bay. Here, in 1745, Bonnie Prince Charlie landed from France in his attempt to gather the clans for his rebellion.

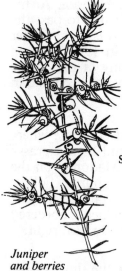

Prince Charlie's Bay

Return to the road and walk on. Look for small falls tumbling down the craggy slopes on your left. Here grow willow, juniper and aspen. Stonechats dart about the bracken tops. Follow the road as it swings right to the side of a small jetty on the side of a bay, which thrusts in from the east coast. Belted Galloways feed on the green slopes and Ben Stack (403 feet) towers above, its dark sides reflected in the silvery water.

Walk back along the narrow road and, when at the top of the hill and beyond the gate taken earlier, climb right over the rocky outcrops and grassy hollows. Head for a gate in the wire fence that runs across the moorland. Once over the gate, climb a grassy gully almost to the top of Ben Scrien (609 feet). Just before the summit, bear right to avoid a very wet area and then climb the easy slope to the triangulation point on the top.

Juniper and berries

From here there is a wonderful view down to the harbour, with its causeway and the colourful houses of the island scattered across a green apron. South Uist lies across the sound, revealing its wide stretch of machair, which suddenly changes

122

into heather moorland slopes. South Glendale and North Boisdale can be seen. In the distance stands Ben Mhor. Out to the east you can see Macleod's Tables on Skye.

Head west, towards the Politician below, dropping down another grassy gully. At the fence walk right to another gate, which you climb. Walk across the rough pasture towards the road — sampling the Politician's wares, if you wish, before catching the ferry. From the garden of the public house you can see two of the white Eriskay horses tethered, which once were used to bring in the peats.

Information

Distance: 5 miles
Time: 5 hours
Map: Landranger 31 reference 789121 (jetty)
Terrain: Easy walking for most of the way. The ascent of Ben Scrien is easy climbing.

35. A Linear Walk from North Glendale

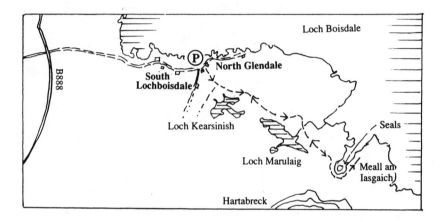

To reach North Glendale, leave the B888 at the signposted turn for South Lochboisdale. Drive along the narrow road, from where there are good views of Loch Boisdale with its many

Loch Boisdale from North Glendale

islands, and on to the end of the tarmac. Park in a large lay-by beyond a new bungalow. Here on the telegraph wires a large number of twites collect after dancing and wheeling over the moors, twittering as they fly.

Walk on along the reinforced track, which is bordered with field gentians, to a gate that is sometimes closed. Immediately beyond, turn right to climb an indistinct track up the slope. Continue uphill to a gate, pass through and swing left to reach another gate. Once through this, bear right uphill, with the fence to your right. Follow the fence as it swings left to pass through a gate onto the moor.

Bear right to pick up an indistinct track used for cutting peats. This leads into a large peat hag, which requires some hump-hopping. Then a very good track starts, and continues distinctly and pleasingly for the whole walk. The track runs in an easterly direction for 200 yards, above Loch Kearsinish. The beginning of the walk is difficult in that the gates through the fences onto the moorland are confusing and the track is almost lost in the peat. But it is a pity to let this deter you from a good walk. If you cannot find the track, aim for the loch and you should see it snaking away across North Glen Dale.

The track passes through heather and bog myrtle and is generally dry. Grouse feed quietly on heather shoots and care for their young. In the distance to the right you can see Loch Marulaig sparkling in its grassy plain and a heron flies down to feed. To the right rears Hartabreck and in the distance you can see the jagged tops of Meall an Iasgaich. When you reach the burn that flows out of Loch Marulaig, you will perhaps find the bridge still down. If so, walk right to a small causeway of boulders across the peaty stream. After heavy rain, the boulders can be underwater, so take care crossing because they can be very slippery. If you find it impossible to cross, end your outward journey here.

Beyond the delightful heather-bordered, reedy stream, continue along the track, from where you can see and hear grey-lag geese. The good track winds on past a lochan on the right and then a larger one on the left. Stride on to the sea inlet of Hartavagh where, on rocks of the lonely bay, under the shadow of Iasgaich, grey seals bask. The track leads to several ruined blackhouses.

Return the same way to rejoin your car.

Grey-lag geese

Information

Distance: *6½ miles*
Time: *3-4 hours*
Map: *Landranger 31 reference 792177 (parking)*
Terrain: *Once on the track, good walking all the way. A few wet patches to be negotiated.*

36. A Walk through East Gerinish to Loch Skipport

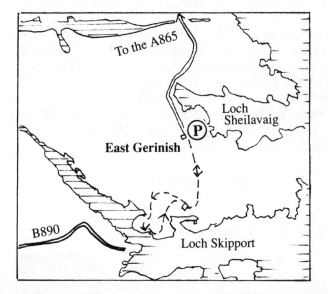

Leave the A865 at the signposted turn-off for Lochcarnan. This is the second turn left, if travelling south, after crossing the causeway from Benbecula to South Uist. Drive along the narrow road, passing a large fish farm, an oil storage depot and a power station, and on to the end of the road. Park neatly in a grassy lay-by close to the sea loch, Sheilavaig.

Walk ahead along a wide grassy track, keeping to the left of a modern house and an old crofthouse. The track moves out into glorious heather moorland, with the Hecla range of mountains ahead, wreathed in mist. Where the track comes beside an inland loch, ignore a left turn and continue past peat cuttings. On an island in the middle of the loch, honeysuckle flowers and willow and heather grow. Ravens fly overhead, croaking gutturally.

The track runs beside a ruined crofthouse that overlooks an inlet of Loch Skipport, and then swings right past an area with sturdy walls, now crumbling in places. These walls surrounded the school, now just a few stones but with steps and gates intact, when the area supported a largish population. One family who lived here sent 13 children to the school.

Stride on along the raised track as it continues over the wet moorland. Just before a rusty gate in a fence, follow the track as it swings uphill towards the ruin of another dwellinghouse that provides a grand view of Loch Skipport and the enclosing mountains. Notice the lazy-bedding running down to a bay on the loch. Strike across the moorland on an indistinct track (west) towards another crofthouse. Here a small stone barn has a roof thatched with heather.

Thatched outbuildings, East Gerinish

Face the dwelling and leave by a causeway on the right. This skirts a craggy outcrop lush with heather, ferns and rhododendrons. Keep to the raised path as it swings right and then left, dropping downhill to a small bay opposite a jetty and a fish farm on the opposite bank of Loch Skipport. Walk left round the low headland, using good sheep-tracks through the heather. When you come opposite a derelict pier with a splendidly-walled access track, move inland for a short distance.

Then continue with the lovely sea loch to your right, still making use of sheep-tracks. Notice the many small inlets, most of which have an old boat still moored. Eventually you reach the ruins of the old school and here can pick up the grassy track that will enable you to rejoin your car.

Polypody and spleenwort

Information

Distance: *3½ miles*
Time: *2-3 hours*
Map: *Landranger 22 reference 835402 (parking)*
Terrain: *Good track for most of the way. No footpaths round the little headland but follow the edge of the loch.*

37. A Circular Walk from Eoligarry Jetty, Barra

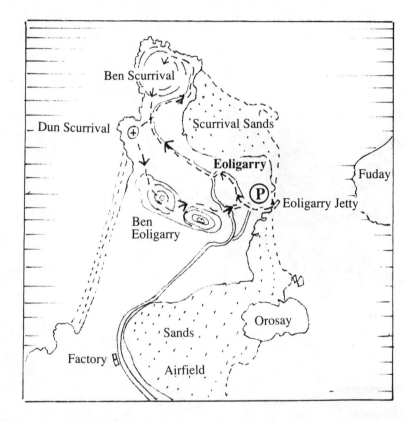

Leave Castlebay by the A888, driving east. After a mile, look for the statue of a Madonna and Child on the slopes of Mount Heaval. Continue along the road for three miles to pass the church of St Barr at Northbay. Here on a promontory into Hirivagh Bay, close to the church, stands a statue of the Celtic missionary, St Finbar, holding aloft a crook.

Take the right turn, signposted Eoligarry, and drive alongside the Tràigh Mhór, an enormous sandy strand used by Loganair as an airfield. Out on the strand people collect cockles and many of these are processed at a small factory on the shore. The ground shell is used for roughcast on house walls and is added to hen feed. The factory was once the home of Sir Compton Mackenzie, who wrote the book *Whisky Galore* based on the shipwreck of the *SS Politician*.

Continue to the cemetery, Cille-bharra, where you turn right and drive for half a mile to Eoligarry jetty car park. A passenger ferry runs from here to Ludag on South Uist. Look across the sands and blue water to Fuday island, where sheep graze. Look for the oyster-catchers, curlew, dunlin and turnstones on the sands of

A turnstone on the sands

Cille-bharra and the cattle feeding on scattered tufts of grass.

Walk back along the narrow lane, which is covered with sand blown from the beach. Turn right at the branching of the narrow road and then on, taking the next right turn. Stride to the end of the road at Scurrival Point, overlooking the sandy bay of Scurrival.

Pass through the gate at the end of the road. Along the indistinct path, tansy and buttercups create a golden glow. Once through the next gate, follow the narrow path over the flower-spangled sward and pass through two more gates. Climb the easy slopes of Ben Scurrival to reach the triangulation point.

The view from the top must be one of the best in the British Isles. Glorious sands stretch for miles. A green sea merges into purple and cobalt blue. Prince's beach on Eriskay (see Walk 34)

131

The view from Ben Scurrival

seems just a short swim away, together with the island's Ben Scrien and Ben Stack. The houses of Ludag and the machair and mountains of South Uist lie to the north. Further away, the mountains of Skye and of the mainland stand out clear in the crystal air. Close at hand Greian Head (see Walk 38) reveals its precipitous cliffs.

Drop down the south slope over outcrops of gneiss to a gate onto the road and walk right (south). Pass through the next gate on the right and climb the slopes to see the Iron-age fort, Dùn Scurrival, its wide flat top just a tumble of rocks from where there is a spectacular view.

Descend the south slope of the hill and begin the ascent of Ben Eoligarry (338 feet). Four buzzards rise and fall with great ease and apparent pleasure on the upwelling air currents. Notice the enormous number of primroses that seem to clothe the slope from top to bottom. From the summit you might see an aircraft land and take off from the sands below and if the tide is out look for tiny figures collecting cockles.

From the top, you have a good view of the narrow strip of dunes that separates the shell-sand bays of the Tràigh Eais and the Tràigh Mhór and you might ponder on how long it will take for the sea to overwhelm the narrow stretch of land. Leave the summit by the eastern slope and descend to a gate at the far right of the cemetery at Cille-bharra. Pass through the gate and turn left. After a few yards, take the gate on the left to visit the cemetery (no dogs allowed).

Cille-bharra, a 12th-century church, has two chapels, one of which has been re-roofed. In the latter are mediaeval carved tombstones and a replica of a runic stone — the original is in a museum in Edinburgh. It has been suggested that the stones from St Finbar's cell (sixth century) were used in the building of Cille-bharra. Sir Compton Mackenzie is buried in this sunny, sheltered, peaceful corner of Barra.

From the cemetery, follow the signpost directions for the jetty and the car park.

Information

Distance: *4½ miles*
Time: *3-4 hours*
Map: *Landranger 31 reference 713077 (parking)*
Terrain: *Easy walking all the way.*

38. A Walk to Greian Head, Barra

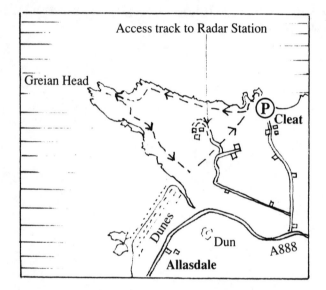

Drive west and then north along the A888 from Castlebay. Turn left at the signposted narrow road to Cleat. Park just before the end of the road on a grassy verge on the right. Walk on and step over the small wall edging the beach to pick up a narrow path. Follow this as it winds round a small bay to an ingenious stile over a fence.

Follow the fence up the slope, moving inland to avoid the edge of the steep cliffs, where fulmars and guillemots fly just above your head as they come into their nesting sites.

View of Greian Head from Ben Scurrival

Continue over the flower-spangled turf, with the reassuring fence between you and the glorious indented coastline. The green sea is streaked with purple. On one of the crags shags perch in an orderly line.

Stroll with care around the headland until you reach a fence. Follow it left to a gate, which you pass through. From here you can walk to Greian Head, where more fulmars nest. Look for field gentians and cowberry with large red berries. Enjoy the vast expanse of ocean.

Cowberry

Return to the gate, or a stile to its right, to recross the fence and walk ahead, along the southern edge of the little peninsula. Your route — there is no path — continues over lazy-beds where oystercatchers pipe and preen. Keep well up the slopes to avoid an area where the sea has eaten into the low cliffs. Stride ahead now, with a good view of the lovely sandy bay of Allasdale and its cemetery above the dunes.

At this point begin to swing left, following the contours of slopes to cross the access track to the radar station. Walk to the fence across the pasture and follow it left to return to the ingenious stile. Retrace your outward route to rejoin your car.

Take care on the slopes. This walk should not be attempted if there is a strong wind.

Information

Distance: 3 miles
Time: 2 hours
Map: Landranger 31 reference 667048 (parking)
Terrain: Easy walking. Occasional wet areas on the top of the headland.

39. A Walk through the Dark Glen, Barra

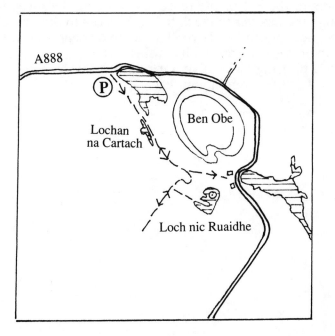

Leave Castlebay and drive east and north along the A888 for seven miles to pass Loch an Dùin. This has been dammed to provide water for the people who live in the northern part of the island.

Park neatly on a grassy lay-by on the left, just beyond the loch. Pass through the gate that has a notice saying 'No dogs beyond this point'. Stroll the wide, easy-to-walk grassy track, passing the silvery loch on your left. Continue on into heather moorland, passing Lochan na Cartach, where water lilies and horsetails thrive. Stride deep into the dark glen.

Go through a gate and over a bridge. The track beyond, now indistinct and wet, leads into a mountain fastness and ends. To the left, beyond the bridge, lies Loch nic Ruaidhe, a lovely stretch of blue water with a dun on its island.

It is possible, at the gate, to follow the stream down the glen, keeping to the left of the fence and walking the sheep-tracks through the heather to reach the A888 close to the old school-house, near Northbay. If you have a kind friend who will pick you up or you can cope with a rather wet ending to your walk, this is a pleasing alternative. Or return from the gate by your outward route to rejoin your car.

Information

Distance: *2 miles to gate and return*
1½ miles from A888 through the glen to the old school-house on the A888
Time: *1 hour*
Map: *Landranger 31 reference 688033 (parking)*
Terrain: *Easy walking to the gate, wet and rough beyond.*

40. A Short Walk on Vatersay

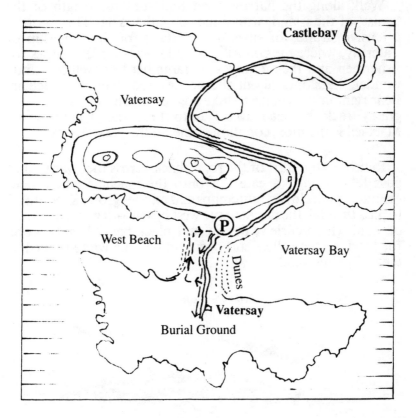

Leave Castlebay by the A888, heading west. Take the third turn on the left, signposted Nask (three-quarters of a mile from the pier). Drive along the new road leading to the causeway that links Vatersay with Barra. It cost three million pounds to build in 1990. Previously, cattle from Vatersay had to swim the often treacherous Sound of Vatersay to reach Barra.

Cross the causeway and continue along the road, which runs above Cornaig Bay, following the coastal road until you pass the school on your right. Just beyond, park on the greensward close to the shop, also on your right.

Walk along the narrow road that runs the length of the 'waist' of the island, with dunes on either side. These border extensive strands of silver sand. Make for the township of Vatersay, where the council has built new wooden houses for fishermen and their families. A large herd of well-fed cattle wander the slopes about the houses and over the machair. Bear right in the village to take a gate on your left. Follow the grassy track that leads to a gate to the burial ground, where MacNeil is the most common name on the gravestones.

Return to the start of the road, back across the 'waist', and pass left through a gate out onto the machair where field gentians, pink clover, buttercups and pansies grow. Keep ahead to pass through the dunes to the west beach — a wide, deep bay of sand where curlew, dunlin and black-backed gulls probe for food. Green rollers curl over and become white-topped as they reach the sand.

Black-backed gulls feeding on the sands

The monument to the Annie Jane

Walk north, almost to the end of the bay, and then pass, right, through a natural break in the dunes. Climb the slope to see a plain monument, a moving tribute to the *Annie Jane,* an emigrant ship that was wrecked in 1853 (the time of the Clearances) with the loss of 450 lives.

Continue on across the machair to a stile to the road. Turn left to rejoin your car.

Information

Distance: *1½-2 miles*
Time: *1½ hours*
Map: *Landranger 31 reference 635954 (school) — those printed before 1990 do not show the new road.*
Terrain: *Easy walking all the way.*

Clan Walks

A series of walks described by Mary Welsh, covering some of the most popular holiday areas in the Scottish Highlands and Islands.

Titles published so far include:

1. 44 WALKS ON THE ISLE OF ARRAN
2. WALKS ON THE ISLE OF SKYE
3. WALKS IN WESTER ROSS
4. WALKS IN PERTHSHIRE
5. WALKS IN THE WESTERN ISLES
6. WALKS IN ORKNEY
7. WALKS ON SHETLAND
8. WALKS ON ISLAY
9. WALKS ON CANNA, RUM, EIGG & MULL
10. WALKS ON TIREE, COLL, COLONSAY AND A TASTE OF MULL

OTHER TITLES IN PREPARATION

Books in this series can be ordered through booksellers anywhere. In the event of difficulty write to Clan Books, The Cross, DOUNE, FK16 6BE, Scotland.